Understanding the Human Mind

Why We Need Thinking Time

Jason Browne

from various sources. Please consult a licensed professional before attempting any techniques outlined in this book.

By reading this document, the reader agrees that under no circumstances is the author responsible for any losses, direct or indirect, that are incurred as a result of the use of the information contained within this document, including, but not limited to, errors, omissions, or inaccuracies.

Table of Contents

Introduction

Louise Hay once said, "Every thought we think is creating our future." There is no greater truth, and thoughts are responsible for who we are, how we act, and whether we're successful in this life. Our thoughts are painting an image from the day we are born, and it's appealing to remain in our comfort zone, no matter how uncomfortable it becomes. However, some of us choose to create a new destiny by shaping the process that controls it all. I assume you are one of us because you are reading this.

Thoughts pop into our minds, and we have little to no control over them. We become vulnerable and helpless toward them when we accept their patterns. We feel like children who are required to listen to our "abusive thoughtful parents." These designs can fail us and lead to physical disease and mental opposition. Nearly every person on this earth wishes to be successful in their life, career, or business, but we feel these intrusive thoughts guiding us on the wrong path. None of us wishes to be in this position. We feel overwhelmed by the power it presents, and we find it difficult to get them back in line. Memories often instigate the negative cycle that takes place in our brain and creates a chain reaction of disaster in our lives.

We feel as though we've lost all control and submit to these interlopers in our minds. They cause us to fail at our targets and even chase our loved ones away. We become alienated, and our minds are seen as strangers. The thoughts run through our minds at a speed that is incomprehensible to the conscious mind. We react inappropriately to a client who sits across the table, or we go off on a tangent with our partner. Our thoughts ignite faster than we can halt them. They embarrass us and cause us to enter a state of negative emergency.

The time has come to end this cycle once and for all. There is a way to take back control of your thoughts before they place you in a hole. Intricate developments are happening in your brain as you read this, and the first thing you need to do is understand them. Your mind soaks up information like a sponge before you can blink. How does one slow down the process of what's happening? How do we become the person we used to be or even want to be?

Science, psychology, and ancient philosophy have given us the answer. Decades of research and trials have provided us the tools we need to stop the flashing images that create havoc in our lives. I'm going to introduce you to sound techniques, and you will build mental acuity, strengthening it further by the day. You can grab the reins from this speedy process and influence the outcome of your future. I will guide you through the biological activities in your brain and give you methods of interrupting them. There are physical techniques to bring you back to a peaceful state where you can govern every response from the thoughts that jump out at you like a deer in headlights.

I've spent years perfecting my advice for people who suffer from their thoughts. You might be wondering who I am and how I could guide you. My name is Jason Browne, and I'm a clinical psychologist who focuses my work on human thought and decision-making mechanisms. I've worked with numerous individual clients, and I've consulted an array of companies and start-up businesses. I pride myself on helping entrepreneurs put together a winning strategy. There's a broad spectrum of barriers that stand in the way of creativity and the limited thinking patterns that most people succumb to. I specialize in strategies to overcome these limitations and expand the mind to new horizons.

There is no need for you to lack creativity anymore or struggle with false corrective persuasions. You should never be inclined to apologize for an outburst of anger or a failure to meet a deadline when your client wants a new presentation. I've written numerous books about self-learning mind control and growing the organ that creates thought patterns. Don't be a prisoner to fly-by-night thoughts anymore but slow time down to pull the strings yourself. You can turn the tables and make this bullet train work in your favor. Join me in this comprehensive guide to the mind, the body, and the correction of frequency. What are you waiting for?

Chapter 1:

The Million-Dollar

Question: How Does the

Human Mind Work?

Answering such an immense question in just one chapter is far from an easy task. The mind or brain is a complexity in all its entirety, but it contains answers to any questions we might have. You have undoubtedly asked the million-dollar question yourself; therefore, I'll shed some light on the intricacies of neural processes, brain chemistry, and all the things that happen for the human mind to function as it does. I'm going to translate the information as plainly as I can because some of it might be difficult to comprehend at first. I know it seemed overwhelming for me before I simplified the processes to my understanding.

The Conscious and Subconscious Mind Revealed

I like to think of the mind as a universe of its own. The universe is vastly misunderstood, and scientists aimlessly attempt to understand it more each day. They've had countless breakthroughs, but as they figure out one item on the list, there's a whole new branch of possibilities that extend from it. Our brains are much the same, and we've come to understand much of it, but there are endless possibilities we are yet to master. Science and psychology can help us learn about what has been discovered thus far and how to shape its development.

Our minds are the very sun in the center of the galaxy, and without its commandments that control each nerve ending in our body, there will be no action, thought, preference, or conversation, among other mechanics. The moment you broke your gaze from these words to process and evaluate the information you've just read was when your brain was firing millions of neurotransmissions and electrical impulses. There's a myth that gets my fire burning inside that says that we only use 10% of our brains. This is far from the truth, and those millions of processes that take place in split seconds contradict the theory. Your brain begins firing on all cylinders as it attempts to make sense of any image in front of your conscious mind, whether it's words you read or words you hear. Sound creates moving images that require information dispensation of their own.

Neurologist Barry Gordon at Johns Hopkins School of Medicine in Baltimore explains that this mythical idea of 10% brain usage is laughable. Gordon expresses the fact that we use nearly every part of our brain and that the majority of our brain is actively operating most of the time. Our gray matter makes up 3% of our bodies in weight but uses an incredible 20% of the body's energy (Boyd, 2008).

Nevertheless, the mind is also considered the judge and jury of every awareness we muster, rational or irrational cognition, and our intelligence. Your conscious sentience and unconscious cognizance influence thoughts, emotions, memory, imagination, will power, and perception. This means that your mind is working during your waking and sleeping stages.

The vast universe that resides in your head is only perceivable by you. You have the potential to gain a somewhat introspective view of all the wondrous communications that take place within your brain. Only you can read your mind, and every thought is familiar to you on some level. There are millions of communicative rivers flowing between the spatial glands and conductors in your mind. One of countless thoughts can penetrate this flow at any given moment.

You find rational thoughts just as you would find distorted thoughts, and perhaps, unwanted and deep-seated thoughts that regulate your physical responses. It's not only the present experience that directs the flow but rather a complexity of ordnance on an endless mound of levels from this viewpoint. These levels correlate to our beliefs, fears, hopes, suspicions, attitudes, motives, and so on.

We all experience an inner dialog that is merely the surface of this dispensing stream that controls the functions of our minds. That inner dialog presents itself as intuition, and the voice inside our minds tells us what to do, think, feel, and expect. It's possible to shift our attention to this intricate flow inside our minds to scrutinize every aspect of the overall process. One should beware of trusting this introspective view, though, when we find distortions and repressed thoughts that often escape us. Various techniques have helped us find our way through the murky deception that could exist in our internal universe.

This universal constellation that regulates our thoughts continues in our unconscious and subconscious minds as we drift through the various levels of consciousness. Each level has its influence and comprises its heights within. Our subconscious mind is one level that can only be reached by introspection into the internal flow of our minds. We cannot reach this directly and require guidance and training to influence it. Your subconscious is widely active during your slow-wave, or delta wave, sleep cycle, and that's why it can be reached if done correctly. We can incept an idea into our subconscious mind to change the patterns of thought when we reach it and put an end to any unnatural brainwaves.

The deeper levels of each conscious plane are filled with all the celestial obstacles that include past experiences and traumatic memories. Those are commonly to blame for our warped flow. The average person is unaware of the way these thoughts infiltrate their stream and impact their conscious thinking.

The History of Exploring and Understanding the Human Mind

The functioning of our brains has been studied closely for longer than the average person knows. This three-pound organ is considered the most complex of them all and contains 100 billion neurons. Studies continue because we need to understand our gray matter to correct it with medication, surgery, treatments, and specialized techniques. Damage to the brain doesn't only come from emotional trauma. Phineas Gage was the reason why physical injury was placed under the microscope in 1848. He was a railway foreman and loved by family, friends, and coworkers. Sadly, he suffered a brain injury at work when a steel rod penetrated the zygomatic arch next to his cheekbone, and he became another person. His entire personality shifted to a mean, profane man. Gage became the frontman for research around an injury to the prefrontal lobe.

However, the story of the brain began before this. Western medicine was still contemplating whether the heart or the brain was responsible for our intelligence by the end of the fifth century B.C. Hippocrates is the first man to have used quotes and phrases that indicated otherwise, circa 460 B.C. to 370 B.C. He often quoted, "Men ought to know that from the brain, and the brain alone, comes our joy, laughter, and pleasures. The same goes for our pain, grief, sorrows, and tears." Hippocrates conveyed a clear message when he spoke about mental functionality and the organ that generates it (Pandya, 2011).

Aristotle lived between 384 B.C. and 322 B.C. and was another philosopher who spoke of the mind. He spoke of a concept called *tabula rasa,* which means that we are all born as blank canvases or states. Experiences and perceptions are written on these blank canvases, and this forms the mind. John Locke is credited with the philosophy even though Aristotle said it first. Aristotle describes the concept in his fourth part of *On the Soul.* The paragraph speaks of the mind being the source of thoughts, and without it, there can be no interaction. These thoughts are much like entries on the blank canvas. He believed that thoughts record themselves on the canvas and dissipate again. This is similar to our modern belief of repressed thoughts.

A long line of philosophers continued to agree and add to the theory of the mind being the center of our existence. Some of these scientists and philosophers included Avicenna (981-1037), Thomas Aquinas (1225-1274), John Locke (1632-1704), and Sigmund Freud (1856-1939). Some names are synonymous with mind and thought processes to this day.

Charles Scott Sherrington, a British man who was considered both a philosopher and scientist, is known for exploring the design of the brain and all its placements in the early 20th century. He found that the mind is buried deep within the brain, where it is furthest away from the outside world. Locke came up with the new concept that the mind cannot be a blank slate because something has to be recognized for it to function as it does in the beginning. He believed that there have to be subtle patterns embedded that are then influenced by other patterns through experience. This is very well part of the argument in nature versus nurture debates. Locke concluded in *The Understanding* that the mind is a complex interaction of multiple parts.

Neurologists and neurosurgeons are specialists who are tasked with correcting matters of the brain. They attempt to restructure faulty compositions in the internal organs of damaged or contaminated brains. Neurosurgeons delve into the physical aspect of the brain and have conducted countless surgeries, learning more with each one. It's common for the patient to be awake during surgery so that they can continue to evaluate the acuity of the person as they tamper with the sensitive organ. The 100 billion neurons are connected to another 100 trillion synapses. These consist of complex human experience and memory. It has been studied and confirmed that when a part of our gray matter dies completely, it no longer exists. It cannot be resuscitated or regenerated again. Damage without natural division in the cerebrum, for example, will remove our ability to speak. Only live gray matter can construct more before it dies.

Doctor Wilder Penfield (1891-1976), a Canadian neurosurgeon, is widely known for his work on stimulating certain regions of the brain with electrical stimulation. He is remembered for his work on epilepsy, but he found that stimulation in certain areas can help someone recall memories they thought they'd lost. Even the thoughts and emotions that originally accompanied the memory were brought to the surface. This was a profound discovery for science and psychology.

Roger Sperry won the Nobel prize for physiology and medicine in 1981 with his groundbreaking work on the two hemispheres in the brain. Sperry studied the confines of splitting the mind in two when he halved the corpus callosum in the brain of a cat. The cat, who now had two separate hemispheres in its brain, showed signs of having two minds. Both halves were capable of learning and retorting intelligently to changes. Studies evolved to the human brain, and the subject was called *John Doe*. Numerous doctors studied the effects of the right and left John Doe's. They showed signs of being identical twins in some aspects and displayed similar personalities. The difference came in the two expressing themselves. John Doe left could convey a language and was better at planning and thinking logically. John Doe right came across as aggressive, impulsive, frustrated, and emotional. Sperry had one conclusion to these studies: slitting the physical brain is a means of splitting one's self. Each hemisphere is responsible for its own thoughts, perceptions, memories, and emotions.

I've included some of the historical timelines because they intrigue me, but there is more to the science and psychology of the brain. I did mention that it would be impossible to cram it into one chapter. I'm sure you understand how far back our research goes now and how it will continue developing for years to come.

Understanding Brain Chemistry

I want to share the anatomy of the brain with you so that I can refer back to a word here and there without causing confusion. I'll use a language that's easy to understand. Our brains are made up of this neural network, to call it plainly. How is this network influenced though? We will have a higher understanding if we know where the main characters are in play and what their purposes are.

I'm sure you're accustomed to the images of this walnut-shaped, colorless organ that has many crevices and folds. There are four main regions in your brain, and the outer, upper layer is known as the cerebrum or upper brain. This is where your two hemispheres meet, and it's covered with an intricate network of nerve cells called the corpus callosum. Each hemisphere has six lobes or sections, and this is where your actionable responses and senses originate. The cerebrum controls your every movement, whether you're conscious or unconscious. It also regulates emotions, speech, intelligence, hearing, and memory. The left hemisphere controls speech and theoretical thoughts, while the right influences spatial thoughts and image creation. The right hemisphere controls the left side of the body, and the left hemisphere controls the right side of the body (How Does the Brain Work, 2018). The cerebral cortex is the region at the upper backside of the hemispheres, and the left is responsible for language, whereas the right regulates spatial compounds. The right side tells you where your hand is at this moment.

The diencephalon is the innermost part of your brain, which houses the pituitary gland, hypothalamus,

thalamus, and pineal gland. It's also often referred to as the interbrain. The thalamus receives signals from your senses and relays it to the cerebrum. The hypothalamus is responsible for what you feel and will communicate the need for sleep, hunger, and thirst, among other things. It works hand-in-hand with the pituitary gland to conduct the symphony of hormones in your body.

The brainstem is the midbrain and consists of pons and medulla that link the brain's network to the rest of the body. It sends communications from the cerebellum to your spinal cord and controls your eye movements and facial expressions. The spinal cord is made up of millions of nerve cells that correlate to every detail in your body. The brain stem is crucial to your breathing, heartbeat, and blood pressure. The cerebellum is located under the backend fold of the brain and is a large region that acts as a support between the brain and spinal column. It's responsible for maintaining harmoniously balanced communications through the neural transmission network. Adrenaline, serotonin, dopamine, endorphins, and enkephalins are all chemicals that pass through this network.

The conscious mind is regulated by hormonal and neurotransmission signals that act as instructions for the release of certain chemicals in the brain and body. The pineal gland instructs the hypothalamus, which then sends neurotransmitters to various parts of the brain and body. These signals are what drive our sleep patterns by releasing chemicals back into the neuro-stream, such as serotonin. This chemical also connects us to our creative side. Dopamine is the feel-good natural drug, and the instructed production of this can regulate our emotions before our thoughts take over. Cortisol is another chemical that passes through the neuro-network, and this is an automatic stress response. Gamma-aminobutyric acid (GABA) is a neurotransmitter that inhibits unwanted thoughts.

The Mind and Soul

All the factors in this chapter have taught us that the brain is where the mind resides because it acts as the control center for your entire body. The mind cannot be allocated to one specific region in your brain because the system as a whole can't function if one part is non-operational. Even though the prefrontal cortex in the front of your cerebrum requires development to create a self, or mind, in certain terms, each cog in the machine is required for the mind to function as a whole. One region might have a greater influence than another in some hierarchy, but the fact remains that they need to work together. We can say that the mind is born in the prefrontal cortex, but it doesn't particularly reside in that region alone. Our sensorimotor development is how we learn to walk, talk, and think. The prefrontal lobe drives this motor as it develops. The mind is the manifestation of this hierarchy level of consciousness. Our senses allow us to experience circumstances or an event and another part of our brain processes the information into thought production in the cerebrum. These processes are a united front that work together to create a result.

The mind is a fascinating subject, but what about the soul? It's another hot topic of discussion among psychologists, scientists, and the average Joe. Socrates explained that we cannot understand the nature of our soul without becoming familiar with our entire body. Ancient Indian philosophers called the soul the *atman*. The search for its whereabouts has been underway since Indian philosophy mentioned it thousands of years ago. We think of the soul as a separate entity from ourselves, and many people believe it to be immortal.

Questions have included when the soul enters the body, whether it defines our intelligence, and if it is related to our conscience. Hippocrates teaches us that madness originates in the brain, but Plato describes it as an ailment of the soul. Pythagoras expressed his ideas of the soul pertaining to intelligence, rationality, and motivation. You can understand why there was much debate about the mind being in the heart or brain now.

Leonardo da Vinci exclaimed that the soul lies within the third ventricle near the corpus callosum in our brains. Many other philosophers and scientists have claimed that the soul lies within the deepest parts of our brain, protected from external sources. This brings about the question; what does life mean? Life begins when the first electrical current runs in the brain, and our soul surely has to be present when life begins. The soul isn't a physically tangible object that can be seen or touched. Neuroscientists have expressed the fact that the soul must reside in the brainstem because it is what links our brain to the body beneath it. When this connection is lost, or our consciousness is lost in brain dead situations, the soul is lost too.

The bottom line is that religious philosophy and science will have various definitions of the location, and we are yet to find evidence of the exact location. The works of various medicinal science practitioners such as William James, Duncan MacDougall, Max Baff, V.S. Ramachandran, Kenneth R. Miller, Christopher Pallis, and Thomas Browne, among others strongly believe that our soul resides in the brain, as our minds do.

Surprising Facts

I can't possibly fill your brain with all this technical jargon without giving you some interesting facts as well. Let me dish them out for you.

Growth and Volume

The human brain can increase in size by up to three times in the first year of your life. The physical brain continues to grow in size until you're 18 years old. Your brain begins to lose some memory abilities and cognitive skills by the time you reach your late 20s. It starts losing its physical size when you cross the threshold of middle age.

Chronic Stress and Shrinkage

This is a scary thought because life is filled with stressors, and it's a known fact in psychology that chronic stress can shrink your brain. Stress is the most influential denominator in brain activity. Prolonged stress affects your brain long-term and physically alters the size of it. The hippocampus is another integral part of the interbrain and is responsible for attention, perception, learning, word-finding, and short-term memory.

People who suffer from chronic stress experience changes in their body that impact the hippocampus and the neurotransmissions in their brain. A lack of sleep, poor nutrition, and emotional distress are linked to the release of glucocorticoids. One of these neurotransmitters is cortisol, and the overproduction of this chemical causes a constant state of panic. This imbalance prevents nerve cells from using crucial nutrients, such as sugar and protein.

The excessive prolonged presence of adrenaline and cortisol in your system will give your midbrain the means to take over, and your prefrontal cortex won't have control over thoughts and decisions anymore. Rats who've been placed under immense stress for a long time displayed a size decrease in the hippocampus.

Nap Time

Sleep has always provided restorative time for our brains, and this goes for brief naps as well. What happens in the brain while we sleep? The majority of the world is right-handed, and that makes the left side of their brain more dominant. However, the right side remains dominant in sleep cycles for both left-handed and right-handed people. Our dominant left hemisphere hands over to the right side when our brains surf the delta waves of slow-wave sleep. Your left hemisphere goes into a recuperative state, and your right side takes charge.

The right side is responsible for moving temporary memories and storage over to the permanent storage and embedding the happenings of the day. This is how we solidify new memories, and this, among other factors, can also play a moving image in our minds when we dream. The moving of information also helps you attain new knowledge when the temporary bits are thrown out. The bottom line is that this cycle that takes place when you sleep, whether through the night or a short nap, improves both memory and learning abilities.

Rewiring the Brain

Another practice used by psychology and modern medicinal techniques is meditation. It's an ancient practice that comes from Hinduism and has traveled its own path through the ages. Meditative practices and mindfulness have influenced religion, science, and is commonly used for leisure purposes today.

Let's step back to stress and anxiety in particular. Meditation has been used to treat anxiety, depression, and stress for many years. The prefrontal cortex takes center stage here again because it relates to how we see ourselves and the experiences around us: perception. There's usually a strong connection between the prefrontal cortex and the body's sensations and fear centers. Meditation teaches us to reduce the strength of this connection, even in the beginning. This practice helps us remove the emotional link to the prefrontal cortex and redirects it to rational thinking.

Meditation helps the mind develop a higher tolerance for stressful situations and makes us see reason in our thoughts, behaviors, and emotions. Besides, mindfulness has been used to enhance our creativity, improve memory skills, and increase the volume of gray matter in our brain. Ancient philosophy speaks of bringing the mind to a present state because living in a different timeline distracts our thoughts and processes. We get to see a situation for what it is in the here and now when we enter a mindful state. Mindfulness is also associated with reaching a higher consciousness, such as the subconscious mind. Reaching the subconscious mind while you're awake is exactly how to retrain your brain because you plant the seed deep enough.

The Aging Mind

The world is plagued with all these horrible diseases, such as Parkinson's, dementia, and Alzheimer's. It's an inevitable truth that our brains will age with us. I've mentioned how the brain starts shrinking after your 40s. The prefrontal cortex reduces in size and capabilities. We know that our memory and higher thinking take place in this region of the brain, and aging causes a vast array of issues. The shrinkage isn't the only culprit here because cholesterol and wear and tear impact our vascular system, which carries oxygenated blood to the brain, among other regions. The brain becomes deprived of oxygen-rich blood as your blood vessels deteriorate over time, and the balance of neurotransmitters is offset. Physical aging can be slowed with the right nutrition, exercise, and the moderation of substances that harm the brain.

Memory, in particular, is a concern in the aging brain because it can affect your thought patterns. There is a decline in neurons and synapses as cells begin to die during aging. This prevents the signals from reaching their destination, and the brain becomes unable to move the older memories and information into permanent storage.

Our brains contain both white and gray matter, and the white matter declines with age. White matter is the insulation that surrounds all nerve cells in the brain. Lesions begin to form on the white matter, and they offer little to no protection anymore. The entirety of the declining process can affect your thought patterns and cause cognitive distortions in your brain. Neurotransmitters are essential to the functionality of the brain, and when this slows down, it forms indistinct responses in thoughts because your thoughts derive from reasoning. You know that your rationality is located in the prefrontal cortex, and when this shrinks and deteriorates, it becomes harder to think realistically.

Chapter 2:

The Birth of a Thought

What is a thought, and how does one suddenly appear in our heads? Very few people have taken the time to ponder this question and uncover how this complex mechanism operates. This process is the one that connects the mind to the brain, human physiology to the thing that makes us unique. Perhaps our soul is what makes us unique. This chapter will examine interesting theories and some scientific evidence about the thought process and the birth of an idea.

The Definition of a Thought

The birth of thought can seem like an alien idea. Have you ever given thought to where it begins? Well, guess what? You're thinking about my question right now because I've ignited a deliberation in your mind. I'm heading into some further jargon to clarify the answer to this question because both Google and the dictionary give vague answers. Vague descriptions don't help us find the deeper levels of answers we need to understand and correct the problem that so many of us face.

Thoughts are reflections of something that we've experienced. It's a tangible process inside the brain that correlates to a likeness of something, such as images, molds, or familiarities that have caught the attention of our sensory receptors in the brain. These similarities relate to something that lies deep within our memory. I've given you examples of how the left and right hemispheres sort memories between your temporary and permanent storage, but now I'll elaborate on what these storehouses are. The permanent storage units are, in fact, your 100 billion neurons that exist throughout your entire nervous system, including the prefrontal cortex. They house luggage compartments on each one of them. They contain synapses, or receptors, that latch onto a memory or likeness to keep it.

These synapses transmit communications through your neural-network by passing them on to the next. You can visualize them as stringed fibers attached between the nerve cells that run through your system, linking them together in a chain-like manner. Memories are dissolved into thousands upon thousands of particles that exist in each receptor. These particles form a pattern that is familiar to your brain specifically. You can think of these particles as fragments or pixels, and they are physical formations. A memory is, in fact, a physical object of information. A thought cannot occur without these pixels forming a whole mental image in your brain. This information-pixelation is accumulated throughout your life and attach themselves to your neurons. Your neurons act as an information highway where all neurotransmitters travel to other regions. Every synapse is activated as the signals pass through.

A thought is created when you experience a collection of activations in these fragmented patterns. The image that comes into your mind and is often called your inner voice is the thought that places these pixels into one unified image. It's a brief burst of physical energy from the brain processes taking place when these fragments come together. Some call it an expression of multiple non-conscious neural activities. It happens so fast that we often fail to notice the creation.

Einstein taught us that energy and mass are interchangeable when he presented his theory of $E=mc2$. Thoughts are waves of energy that resonate through our system, and therefore, they are interchangeable with mass. Neuroscience continues to study the complexities involved in our thought processes because it remains a mystery to some extent. The best explanation they offer presently is that it's a brief conscious expression of these brain activities. There isn't viable evidence of what stimulates this brain activity other than encouragement by our five senses. A thought can also be referred to as a response to these charges, and because it happens below our level of consciousness, it's classified as automatic.

Your senses play a major role in what's happening at any given moment. This includes audio, sight, smell, taste, and touch. You walk into a room where there's an apple pie in the windowsill. and the sight of the kitchen table combines sensual stimuli to surface the thought of your grandmother. Immediately, you lick your lips because "Gran" made the best apple pie you ever had. You can suddenly feel the texture on your tongue and taste the perfect balance of sweet and tangy simultaneously. There's a flood of emotions that accompany the situation, and a thought pops into your mind. The experience that birthed the thought was walking into the room, and the stimulus in the room has tickled your senses and built a mental image. This mapping of memory fragments relates to emotions and thoughts you've previously felt in similar moments that created the pixels in the first place. The emotions involved could be positive or negative, and so can the thought itself.

It gets a little more complicated though. During the process where your right hemisphere stores these fragments in your neurons, it doesn't store them all in one place. The concept of having all your ducks in one pond is foreign in your neural system due to its vast complexity. One memory can be spread over many of the 100 trillion synapses along your highway. More complex is the fact that a particular particle of likeliness can move between neurons and even reshape the cell it latches onto entirely. This explains why we experience déjà vu in a place we've never been to. It's an accumulation of numerous fragments that have electrically fired together to create one similarity. This can become a pattern when these neurons are constantly firing together. Our entire nervous system is the network in which these synapses travel consistently. The reason we can feel a thought is because we are housing the information that provides the thought. It's a non-stop highway where information never halts, even when we sleep.

The Thought Retaliation Process

This response that we call a thought has its own hierarchy of influence over various other processes in our system. Our emotions are directly connected, and we can feel fear, sadness, stress, and even fatigue. Emotions and thoughts derived from beliefs that were created in our fragments over time can be a recipe for an explosive response. Neurotransmitters are released the moment your body draws an emotional reaction from your thought, and these chemical messengers release hormones that wreak havoc in your system. On the other hand, it can also relay the release of dopamine or serotonin to calm you down and make you wish to taste a slice of that apple pie in the windowsill.

Unfortunately, the actionable responses that come from our emotions can be negative. You might be feeling down because your grandmother passed away recently, and fragments from this memory are seeping into your thoughts, intoxicating them. You can call this automatic negative thoughts, or ANTs. Now your brain releases chemicals such as cortisol as a response to stress. Your adrenaline rises, and your actionable response might be tears. I'm trying to explain how ANTs or any automatic thought could control your behavior in one swift moment. The chemicals that travel through your body even latch onto the endocrine system, and your digestive system can suffer. Have you ever felt that deepening black hole that forms in your gut when you're anxious? It's just another physical response to the thinking process.

Our automatic thoughts are so powerful that they influence any reaction in us. Let me explain the power that lies in our thoughts. Think about the question of believing what you think for a moment. Let's discuss the placebo effect to convey the message because it's commonly used in the medical and psychological field and proves just how powerful our conscious thoughts can be. Patients have been prescribed medication or led to believe they experienced some form of surgery when indeed, the medication was fake or reference to the surgery contained no details of what was done. The patient will continue consuming the medication with the belief that it is used for depression, but it's actually just a multivitamin. The person's thoughts are so incredibly powerful that they feel improvement in their life.

The placebo effect isn't only used in psychology but has been successful in fitness and even physical strength training. We can deceive our thoughts and use them to our advantage to change the way we feel and respond. I've used this in my practice because it proves effective in many cases and can often reveal the strength of thoughts to my patient. Long periods of certain behaviors and thoughts shape your brain into a specific form due to the magnitude of influence they have. The receptors on each neuron consist of certain peptides or proteins. A peptide is an amino acid or an exact likeness accumulation of neuropeptides. Depression, for example, releases chemical neuropeptides in your system and begins to permanently alter the form of your receptor. This is why you find it easier to be depressed when you've been depressed for a long time.

The afflicted neuron will divide from the others to accommodate excess information and will contain these faulty peptides or receptors. It will fail to contain the receptors required for latching onto emotions and thoughts you haven't exposed yourself to frequently. This confirms that the alteration of thoughts over a prolonged period can shift the balance in our brain. The more you feed them with negativity, the more negative they'll become.

Your thoughts even sway your genes. Life experience isn't the only culprit that shifts genetic factors in your life and predisposes you to negative responses; it's the teaching of negativity to your genes. Your nerve cells are chopping and changing, and that also pulls strings with your genetics. The link between genetic issues and health disorders is merely 5%. The remaining percentage goes to your mental acuity. This means that the influence from your thoughts and responses can inadvertently shift the genetics in your body.

Perception and thoughts are what drive the responses in you; therefore, only you can take control of them. They direct your biology, and every time you snap at a loved one, it's a distorted thought that's to blame. The good news is that you can control the genetic influence of your brain. The connection between your mind and body is irrefutable. Mindfulness takes the reins here because it allows you to enter the subconscious mind and take back the steering wheel. Various treatment options that relate to the brain can help you regain control over it.

We need to start at the beginning to alter the end result, and memories are the culprit because they decide how we think. Our thoughts can constructively or destructively alter our nerve cells or neurons. Our bodies are incredible packages of splendor because there's one more fact I can share with you. The reason you can rewire your brain doesn't only lie in philosophical methods and explanations; it also lies in science. The human body goes through a cycle of changes every two months. The nerve cells along our network die buy generate new cells before they do. That's why we can change our reality and thought processes. Yes, the fragments that travel between the nerve cells exist, some permanently and others temporarily, but we can replace the host that houses them with one that contains the desired receptors.

Our brains are highly adaptable, and new synapses are born to handle any excess or new information they need to pass on. The receptors on your network multiply when there is a frequent activity in one area of the brain or a collection of fragments frequently activate at once. Let's use an example of how these synapses and networks grow to accommodate the additional volume. Imagine you're a cab driver in New York and that this has been your profession for years. Your hippocampus will automatically be larger because new receptors and cells have to grow to accommodate the additional mapping of New York City. Fragments of streets and landmarks will create thousands and thousands of pixels that can come together to form an area where you need to go.

The hippocampus is the region where spatial imagery is stored and created. This is another example of power because the brain will continue to accept new information and even grow to house it. There is no reason we can't use the power of our brains to our advantage and replace any faulty processes.

Looking to Science

I'm going to discuss a few studies to enrich your knowledge of how science agrees on the facts I've given you in the previous section. Many of us resist information unless it is proven to us, and I can respect that in my professional capacity.

The first study I'll focus on is where people's brain capacity and general knowledge were increased by using science and psychology. You have to admit that it sounds intriguing because who wouldn't want to know more and come across as an intelligent person? Allow me to rephrase that. Who wouldn't want to become an intelligent person? Psychologists Ulrich Weger from the University of Witten-Herdecke in Germany and Stephen Loughnan from the University of Melbourne in Australia used the placebo effect to trick people into being 'smarter' in a simple test (Weger & Loughnan, 2012). The purpose of their examination was to determine whether we can breach the extent of our knowledge through deception because our brains are capable of more than we know. It's merely a case of allowing our brains to dig into their abilities that they frequently overlook or that we allow them to ignore.

They tested two groups of individuals and placed them in front of a computer screen. One group was asked to answer questions on general knowledge and told that the answers would flash on the screen briefly. This would happen so fast that they wouldn't consciously acknowledge the answers, but they would unconsciously receive them. The second group was given the same test, except the flashing screen was supposedly an interlude to the next question. This is where their belief came into play. The truth about the fast flashing screen was that it contained neither and was merely a flash of randomized letters that did not correlate to the test.

Nevertheless, the first group who believed they had seen the answer excelled on the test overall. The second group didn't do as well as the first. This proves how we can deceive our minds into fetching answers or thinking differently and finding a solution to a problem we thought was insurmountable at first. Our minds are powerful tools and should be utilized to our benefit by encouraging it to work harder and shift thought patterns.

Let's take a look at my "theory" regarding the growing brain because I kid you not, it's possible to make your brain grow larger. There is no reason to limit your brain capacity or abilities. Eleanor McGuire at University College London is a neuroscientist who studied the cab drivers of London over four years (Jabr, 2011). McGuire, along with her colleague Katherine Woolett, studied 79 individuals who inspired to be cab drivers. They used magnetic resonance imaging (MRI) to record and measure the growth of the hippocampus before and after the test.

A total of 31 people were matched intellectually and educationally from within the same age group and who didn't drive cabs were used as a control group for comparison. Every participant had a similar volume of gray matter at the start of their study and showed comparative memory abilities on certain tests. Only 39 of the 79 training cab drivers had earned their licenses four years later. There were 20 people with failed attempts at the career option who continued with the study.

The drivers that passed their training outperformed those who didn't when they were given memory tests again. This means that the official cab drivers had improved over the four-year study. The licensed cabbies also showed an increase in gray matter in the hippocampus region after the study was completed. Howard Eichenbaum, a neurobiologist from Boston University, commended the research and confirmed that cognitive practices can create physical alterations in the brain. This is essential knowledge because you need to realize that you can increase the volume of your brain and make physical changes in its fabric.

There is one more scientific examination I want to share with you because it clarifies much of what I've spoken about. The Max Planck Institute for Human

Cognitive and Brain Sciences has been dipping its feet into research for many years now. It has shared its findings in an article published in the *Journal of Physiology* in 2019 (Nierhaus et al., 2019). This institute used brain-computer interfaces (BCI) to measure the electrical pulse modifications in the brain when thoughts are stimulated. The results are read through an electroencephalography (EEG). These results are evaluated and transformed as control signals through a machine learning system. This can then be used to operate a computer. Yes, I realize this is transferring intelligent information from a human to a computer in its most basic form. Keep in mind that it's for experimental purposes only in this instance.

I apologize for the technical jargon, but it allows us to understand the research better. This study was conducted with partners from the Public University of Navarre and the Berlin Institute of Technology because some technological aspects were beyond the understanding of those at the institute. Nevertheless, subjects were exposed to one hour's training of manipulating electrical pulses in specific regions of the brain, and the results were astonishing. These electrical charges imitated the thought process desired and showed significant changes in the processing of the computer. This means that thoughts are confirmed to alter the structure and functionality of our brain.

I'll focus on the second group of participants that were exposed to visual stimuli on a computer monitor. They were required to recognize and select letters on a screen because this would automatically encourage thoughts. Participants' motor system or senses were used to activate the necessary thoughts in their brain. Our understanding at this point is that thoughts can only be initiated through the senses, as I've mentioned before. The BCI system wasn't used alone, and subjects were examined using a magnetic resonance tomography (MRT) to record the changes in their brains as well in the imaging results. The MRT came to the same conclusion when there were visible changes in the structure of the participant's brains.

Science has given us the ability to delve into understanding the universe around us, and our brains are the center of our universe. Thoughts are unavoidable, and their responses are undeniable. We might still have to pinpoint certain factors in science, but our insight into the human brain and mind is expanding by the day. There is one psychological approach that focuses on the happenings inside our brain.

The Connection Between Cognitive Psychology and Thoughts

People who are unfamiliar with cognitive psychology will wonder how it relates to thoughts and the patterns that take place in our brains. A psychologist who specializes in cognitions will get to the bottom of why a thought occurs in your mind before it's replaced with rational, alternative thoughts. This fairly new era of psychological treatment is aimed at placing your brain activity under the microscope. All these patterns we've discussed are what inspired this treatment method. It looks at perception, memory, thinking, attention, language, learning, problem-solving, and consciousness, which are ignited by these electrical charges in the brain.

Cognitive psychology began in the early 20th century but started gaining profound momentum in the 1960s. Wolfgang Kohler was the first psychologist to reject the idea of behaviorism and delved into the cognitive realm when he observed insightful behavior in monkeys that helped him understand that the processes in our brain influence our behavior. He published the famous book known as *The Mentality of Apes* in 1925. Edward Tolman is another name synonymous with the birth of cognitive therapy. He denied the theory that humans are passive learners and concluded that we are actively processing information all the time, referring back to our mental processes. Tolman supported the idea of behavioral changes through cognitive learning, and his applications are widely used in modern psychology.

George Miller is the name we are most familiar with from the late 1950s. He published a book called *The Magical Number 7 Plus or Minus 2* in 1956 and is often referred to as the father of cognitive psychology. Miller, along with Jerome Bruner, started the Center for Cognitive Studies at Harvard University in 1960. Ulric Neisser published a book called *Cognitive Psychology* in 1967, and this was when the therapy became widely known and practiced. Cognitive psychology influences behavior therapy, developmental therapy, social therapy, and biological science, even though it's a younger participant.

This form of psychology compares the brain to that of a computer just as the Max Planck Institute for Human Cognitive and Brain Sciences do. A computer uses information processing to gather information, transform it, store it, and retrieve it when necessary. Doesn't this sound similar to what you've learned about brain activity? The computer processing approach of cognitive therapy translates to three levels of development.

A computer's memory uses input, storage, and output for every strand of data communication it receives. Input is the stage where stimuli are analyzed. This relates to the stage where your senses receive the data and analyze it with your fragments of memory. Storage can refer to the relocation, manipulation, and coding of the stimuli. This relates to your thinking process. Output refers to the response toward the stimuli. This is when humans become emotional and react to stimuli.

If you notice that manipulation is in the second stage, you'll understand why cognitive therapy takes advantage of the mind's processes to change thoughts and patterns. The only time a thought can be impressed is when it's in the storage process of your brain. We can pinpoint any possible cognitive distortions that regulate our thoughts when we can understand the brain and its working order. This is the precise focus of cognitive psychology. You can even call this therapy a scientific formula of sorts. It wouldn't exist without the scientific and medical research that has taught us about the brain.

Cognitive psychology has been used to differentiate short-term and long-term memory and honed the techniques needed to convince our brains to store memories accurately and even amend their impression on our thoughts. Memories play a role in our thoughts, and learning to change the memory storage capabilities of your brain is the way you alter your thoughts. Short-term memory isn't widely understood, and the definition of it is scary, to say the least. It's a memory that lasts 20 to 30 seconds and usually only contains between five and nine inserts.

Cognitive therapy will focus on finding negative thoughts in particular. It's essential for someone who experiences automatic negative thoughts to correct their issue with cognitive treatments because our thoughts are what control who we are. They drive every response we have, and if we want to be successful in life, we need to conquer them by becoming a master manipulator. Improving your attention is just another reality of enhancing your life because people who suffer from attention distortions find it difficult to cope at work.

Negative thoughts are the largest enemy, though, because of the constant rumination that we live in can disrupt our lives entirely. We can find it difficult to function daily, experience increased stress, learn self-sabotage, and even adopt feelings of self-learned vulnerability. Cognitive therapy will guide you on maneuvering these negative cycles of rumination that live inside your brain and replace them with positive and self-growing thoughts.

This branch of psychology aims at identifying twisted beliefs that are formed with the fragments of memory from our internal storage and replace those beliefs with realistic notions so that we can be the person we need to be. Cognitive psychology has impacted mental health vastly, but it's not only used for patients with mental disorders. It's commonly used for people who want to gain the upper hand on life and defeat any resistance they hold within themselves. The day you recognize your thoughts as being the essence of your failure to succeed is the day you know that cognitive treatment is the specialist approach you need to master.

Chapter 3:

The Importance of Having

More Thinking Time

We live in a very hectic world, and often, decisions are made "on the go." People have very little time to stop, think carefully, and analyze different ideas and outcomes. Our thought processes are rushed, but slow thinking is very important for a couple of distinctive reasons that I'll share with you.

Slow vs. Speedy

Are you aware of the famous "thinking man" statue? The thinker or "Le Penseur," as the French call it, is a bronze statue of a large heroic styled nude man originally modeled from the first statue by Auguste Rodin in 1919. The bronze man depicts a man deep in thought, and the model by Rodin stands in the Rodin Museum in Paris today. Auguste used an athletic man from which the figure was built so that it can convey a message to say that thinking is a powerful tool. I couldn't agree more. Dante Alighieri, a famous Italian poet, was the model for this statue. Poetry finds its inspiration in thoughts. My point is that thinking is the act in which we find our success and has been suggested as such for a long time already.

Humans can think on their feet. It happens so fast that we often don't even realize it's happening. Fast thinking is the automatic spark of cells that light up in our minds, and it takes mere fragments of a second to build an image that we call thought. Fast thinking has been debated for as long as man knew it existed. It benefits our lives in many ways, from personal to business, but it can also be our downfall. Let's use an example of an entrepreneur who owns a fast-food shop.

A customer purchases the cheeseburger special and sits down at a booth. Five minutes later, the customer is frantically raising their voice and sharing the news of the hair they found in their patty with the entire city, never mind the establishment. The smartphone comes out, and the flash lights up as they activate video recording. The entrepreneur who has built this business from the ground up is standing nearby and watching the spontaneous combustion of the customer. Take a moment and think of the customer and acknowledge that this person is experiencing their own fast train of thought and responding uncontrollably. Their voice is carrying over the entire restaurant, and onlookers are staring wide-eyed.

The entrepreneur has a process in their brain that is traveling faster than the speed of light, and all the fragments from their nerve cells are forming an image. They are about to lose all the clients in this restaurant right now, not to mention the word of mouth that will destroy their business. Emotions run wild, and anxiety takes the lead as the sweat pours from their forehead. The entrepreneur rushes over and attempts to calm the customer down. They offer the client compensation and ask them gently to lower their voice.

The owner of this burger joint will do anything to keep the client from upsetting the remainder of their clients further. They are begging the customer to quit their cries and assure them of immediate correction. The reason behind my example is to show you one advantage of fast thinking in the business world. Some circumstances will require swift action, and in this case, the owner's reaction was logical and necessary. However, now the entrepreneur has offered the customer free burgers for a month without negotiating a settlement that would ensure the safety of the business. This customer could still walk out the door and place a review on the internet.

Fast thinking allows us to address problems that need diffusing immediately and is required in some instances; however, we need to tread lightly and use it appropriately. I teach my patients and business clients to make use of another valuable process, known as slow thinking.

People confuse fast and slow thinking because they assume that fast thinking is good. They watch quiz shows on television and find themselves thinking, "Wow, that person is on the ball." Keep in mind that real life isn't a quiz show, and slow thinking or hesitation won't necessarily lose us points. I'll refer to the famous saying that we should think before we speak. Have you never said something and regretted it immediately? I know that I've done this, and none of us are immune to compulsive reactions. Sometimes, we would even believe that our reaction is reasonable in our defense, but the consequences linger from the moment the words leave our mouths.

Neuroscience explains that slowness of thought is an integral part of brain activity. Releasing the perceived emotional response is the first thing our minds do when thought is conceded. We need to interrupt our thoughts before the emotions burst through the gates. It is possible to perceive something as a threat when it actually isn't one. Slowing down our thoughts gives us the opportunity to create opportunity—pun intended.

Referring back to business again, thoughts are ideas, and there's a vast difference between an idea and an opportunity. The moment you slow the process of your neurons down is the moment you find the actions needed to turn an idea into a viable opportunity. It gives you time to accumulate knowledge and all the variables of a situation before you act on the idea. Someone who wants to purchase a product from a new supplier for their business should always consider every variable. They cannot react impulsively because they're saving $0.20 per item from the new supplier. They should take time to think it through and consider why the item is cheaper. Is it of the same quality? Will you lose customers if the quality differs? Thinking time can provide you with the opportunity to gather knowledge about the competitive products for comparison before signing a new supplier erratically.

The same applies to someone who wants to start a new business. They need to give every single aspect thought before they jump into an agreement even if the price entices them like sirens lured the sailors to their ocean death in mythology. It doesn't matter if the offer on the table is for a limited time either because the entrepreneur wants to know all the facts before they lay down their funds.

Where the Mental Processes Lie

Let's spend some time learning about neural activity and what science says again because we can't argue with facts. Mental processing as thought is divided into two sections: fast and slow. Both thoughts and emotions are considered super-fast highways of neuron activity. It makes me think of the Germans because they have autobahns rather than highways. Drivers are required to drive at excessive speeds on these roadways. The advantage is that there are eight lanes in each direction, and if one car is driving at 100 miles per hour, and the other is driving at 50 miles per hour, there's a high probability of an accident. That's why there's a recommended speed limit of 100 miles per hour.

Anyway, science explains the speeds at which your thoughts travel. Scientists use electroencephalography, or EEG, to measure the speed in which your brain activity occurs. They call it neural or brain oscillations and commonly use meters per second (ms) to record how far the electrical activity travels per second. They place electrodes on your scalp to measure the electrical flow. Another version of measurement is called functional magnetic resonance imaging (fMRI). This measures the rate at which your blood flows and activates neurons. The importance of understanding this will help you understand how they've come to the conclusion that thoughts and their emotions that follow travel at 165 meters per second (Kringelbach et al., 2008).

Parental instinct was used to measure these speeds when adults were studied; they were presented with unfamiliar infant faces to stimulate certain thoughts and emotions. Most of us have the indistinct ability to instantly feel emotionally attracted to babies, and our automatic thoughts take over. I know this has nothing to do with business, but I want to use it as an example to show you how fast your thoughts travel. There were a few variables, but the fastest result they recorded was 165 ms.

Cognitive psychology has given us the means to slow down these hasty processes in our brains, and it's called cognitive reappraisal. This technique has been used in cognitive behavior therapy (CBT) and others as well. It aims at teaching us how to pause for a moment and scan through all the details before we allow an emotional response to take the lead. Remember that emotion will follow thought, and unfortunately, it will lead to a response in behavior or even words spoken. I'll use another example here.

There is a meeting in the boardroom, and all parties involved are sitting around the table. The junior partner is itching to share an idea that just popped in their head and waits for the perfect gap. There's a brief pause between presentations, and the junior reacts on their excited thought while the next person links their PowerPoint presentation to the screen. They suddenly blurt their idea out in the open without even asking for their colleagues' attention. Their words are speedy and difficult to follow. Their colleagues raise their heads from their clipboards for a moment, and the boss asks, "What?"

There is a look of confusion across the board, and the boss wears a doubtful look. Immediately, the junior's thoughts are pointing out their failure, and the expressions they see are that of disappointment. They feel gloomy and dismiss the idea they had so much faith in because everyone else thinks it's not worth considering. The problem here is that the junior has given into their automatic negative thought and never spent a moment reappraising it before they shrugged it off. Their colleagues were busy contemplating and making notes on the previous presentation, and the boss only asked "What?" because he didn't hear the junior's interruption clearly.

This is the perfect example of our speedy thoughts deceiving us and giving us the wrong impression. There was no look of doubt on the boss's face. It was merely a question because they heard the junior talking but not what was said. If the junior took five seconds to think reasonably and reassess the situation that triggered the negative thoughts, they would have shared the great idea they had.

Cognitive reappraisal allows us to re-examine the situation and our first thoughtful response before we give way to the emotional reaction. We can even reassess the "trigger" after our initial response. This is also well-known as slow thinking when we take a brief moment to ponder on the circumstances. We are more likely to think rationally when we take this short timeout. The junior might even realize that their response was because they were never appreciated in their previous position. It doesn't mean they aren't appreciated in the new company. The junior's idea might have been valuable, but no one would know anymore.

I'll use a study conducted to use cognitive reappraisal to shift the mood in depressed and stressed people. Both are a good example of how we could allow our thoughts to send us into an undesirable mood, which is highly detrimental in business too. Some people allow their thought patterns and neural activity to drive them into these emotional states, and others build resilience against them. Which do you wish to be? Cognitive reappraisal opens you to a world of emotional regulation.

Allison S. Troy in the Department of Psychology at the University of Denver, along with her colleagues, conducted a study on patients who had been through a recent traumatic event that sent them into emotional dysregulation (Troy et al., 2010). Troy deployed 78 women from the community rather than undergraduates. Participants used a behavioral study and filled out a questionnaire before it began. Each woman was required to record her sadness and then watch a short emotional video. Then, she would record her sadness levels again.

These results remained the same as the first questionnaire, and some were even more devastating. The women were asked to watch another short emotional film and then instructed to reappraise the video after. They chose their sadness levels again, but this time, there was a notable decline. The conclusion was that emotional regulation evaluation gave the women a lower sadness score. Troy gave more examples of a meta-analysis in her article, and multiple studies have shown the same results. People who pause briefly to reassess their trigger event are more likely to cope with the outcome or see a different outcome altogether.

Slow Thinking

There's no doubt suppressing our immediate emotions and looking for reason in our thoughts will take practice. Our brains have functioned at a certain speed for a long time, and we will redirect the flow with practice and persistence. We cannot change the circuitry overnight, but when we do alter it, the variation will give us the upper hand in life and business.

Slow thinking allows us to slow the speed of thoughts running stray in our minds. These thoughts are frequently the culprit of unreasonable images. I know it's difficult at first because we believe that it's like jumping in front of a speeding train. I want to assure you of one thing: Your mind is your own, and you are more than capable of taking back control. Thinking about a stressful situation can help you see things clearly that you might have overlooked before. You can imagine how easy it is to skip a factor when those neurons are lighting up so rapidly.

One pixel of information in your synapses might be missed, and that could be the one that changes the entire analysis. None of us choose to make poor decisions that come from reading part of the story. That flashing image in our minds that we call thought could be missing vital information, and now the image is far from the truth. We need to know the whole story and force our brains into finding the misplaced fragment of memory that's evaded us. This fragment can be lost within minutes or even seconds of experiencing the circumstance. Slow thinking will help us overcome bad decisions based on hasty responses and misinterpretation of the final image in our minds.

Making rapid and inconclusive decisions can lead to stress, even when we're excelling. It's complicated to handle a situation in the business when stress grabs hold of us. It distorts our outlook further, and we become negative in a situation that has a solution. It's not the end of the world when a client purchases a faulty product from our business. There is a solution to every problem; we just need to take the time to search for one that makes us and the client happy. Replacing the product might turn the problematic client into a loyal and frequent shopper.

There are more advantages because when we reassess the factors a second, third, or even a fourth time in our minds, we might find one fragment that enlightens us to new possibilities. This refers to turning an idea into an opportunity again. Human beings find a bottomless well of motivation when they are certain their idea will work. It gives us something to look forward to, and goals are where motivation is born. If we believe in the method of reaching the desired goal, our motivation will ignite like a fire that never burns out. What more could we ask for in business?

The Different Thinkers

Nobel prize laureate Daniel Kahneman has written a book called *Thinking, Fast and Slow*. He has included a premise that fellow psychologists support in his book. Kahneman called Barack Obama a slow thinker. Someone who learns to slow down their network charge will see this as a compliment and not an insult. Some people would be offended by this, but that will indicate that they're speedy thinkers who jump to conclusions. Anyway, psychology divides thinkers into two separate categories. The first is called system one thinkers, and the second is called system two thinkers. I know the names are not very original, but that's just the way it is.

System one thinkers are the people who discard their evaluation of a circumstance and jump on their high horse. I mean no offense, but I call these people slaves to their impulses. They involuntarily hand their control over to the impulsive behavior that often follows automatic thoughts, whether they're negative or positive. These people function in a way that drives them to find the fastest outcome, no matter how unreasonable it might be. They are prone to making bad decisions and have little to no control over the neural network that exists in their minds. You can call these people zombie slaves because the premise of zombies is that they have no control over their impulses. It is, unfortunately, a common human error, and many of us follow this way of life before learning to break through the restraints that accompany our human condition.

The question you need to ask yourself is whether you want to be tied down by such a common problem in society. Many of the people who find themselves stuck in this cycle don't choose it. They don't know any better until someone points out the error in their rapid judgments. People commonly rely on first impressions in business, and when we are stuck in the system one thinking phase, we can lose a client that would have supported us for many years to come. We don't want to jump to conclusions and lose valuable people in our business.

The day we decide to change this is when we evolve into system two thinkers. Obama was called a system two thinker when he was referred to as a slow thinker. Psychologists have often called him a thoughtful man. This may even have something to do with why he spoke so slowly. He had trained his brain to think as he speaks. We enable ourselves to allocate enough attention to mental activities when we slow down the pace. It's a matter of welcoming conscious awareness into our minds and removing the shackles that enslaved us. Our minds are powerful, as you have already learned, and it's simpler than you think to fall under its spell. You've taken the first step by learning about how the mental process begins in your brain and the reaction that follows. Ideas are born in these thoughts, and only we can redirect them into genuine opportunities to excel in our business.

The thesis surrounding the two categories is simple. A system one thinker is impulsive and allows themselves to be emotionally deterred by automatic instincts. A system two thinker makes way for logic and deliberately chooses to question every fragment of thought.

The Business of Slowing Down

I'll say it once more: Modern-day life has become a crazed collection of hectic. Life is busy, especially in the world of entrepreneurship. Business owners are restricted to schedules, budgets, meetings, and a never-ending cycle of running around. The most important factor is to see that the business succeeds at any cost. Many new business owners make the mistake of unintentionally falling into fast thinking because they are overwhelmed and fear the failure of an idea. Their lives fill up with distractions in the form of making sure everything is running smoothly at all times. Failure is the end of the world and must be avoided at all costs. Adrenaline runs high, and cortisol pumps through their veins constantly.

There is nothing easy about starting a new company. It's one of the most stressful times in anyone's life. Our time is of the essence, and we feel that we can only move fast rather than think consciously on our feet. The person has seen a gap in the market, and their ultimate desire is to fill that gap. We allow our hearts to beat at a pace that resembles the drumming of an approaching Vikings ship in the mid-10th century. I'm going to ask you to do one thing right now. Sit back and see yourself in this position where you are running on the last breath in your lungs. Think about the neural processes I've shared with you and acknowledge what's happening in your mind right now. Feel free to spend as much time in this thoughtful moment as best suits you.

Time. It's another undeniably valuable asset. It's one asset that business owners, new and old, see as an irreplaceable substance. I will not argue with the truth because the only thing we can never recover is time.

Yesterday is history, and none of us have built that infamous time machine yet. This doesn't make time an enemy, and this is a common misconception. We run head-first into the day and never give it a second thought. Time is an invaluable and priceless commodity that entrepreneurs can use to their advantage. All they have to do is learn to manipulate time.

How do we do this, you may ask? We combine the ability that gives us a great lead over the competition with time to create a loophole. Providing ourselves with enough time in a distracted world is one of the rudiments of success. We can call it the difference between having the time and doing the time. You don't want to be among the entrepreneurs and busy professionals who fail to find the perfect balance.

The first thing you do is discard any regrets from yesterday. Remember that you'll be wasting time by pondering on a timeframe you can't change. Come to the present time and use meditative practices if you need to hone this ability. Regret, guilt, and uncertainty will all lead to indecisiveness, and you want to bring yourself to the present to avoid this. The only space in time you can alter the path your business takes forward is here and now. There is no other time you can do it. The moment you feel a pessimistic thought pop into your head is the moment you freeze in the present time. You will learn to challenge any thoughts that don't seem kosher at first when you look at it closely. Forget about any influence the past has on your decision or response and delegate every fragment that accumulates to create your image.

There is one incredible ability we all contain within us. This is the talent of creating time for something. We decide when the best time is to sit down and think. I call this thinking time, and without it, how do you suppose you'll conjure up new ideas that turn into million-dollar opportunities? Successful businessmen allocate up to 20% of their time every week to thinking.

Choose an entry in your diary to allocate thinking time for the week. You can even begin with an hour at a time. All the concerns that have bothered you before this silent time can come to the surface now. Don't give your mind the upper hand by allowing it to choose when you think. The negative thoughts that have previously hindered thinking time will be trumped by supplying genuine time to sit and ponder. There should be no meetings, work-related distractions, or even personal amusements at this time. Learn to be confident in being alone and combing through any thoughts that jump out from behind the bushes.

I strongly advise that you keep a record of what you thought and what the results of your alone time were when you are done. This can be some kind of checklist. It provokes motivation in us when we can visualize our progress, and it guides us in finding faulty patterns. I will give you an example in later chapters. If you want to be on the next Forbes list of entrepreneurs, you should most certainly invest in some thinking time.

Chapter 4:

Factors That Impact Your Thinking

To become a more conscious and mindful thinker, you will have to understand the factors that could affect the inner functioning of your brain. This chapter will take a look at some of the most prominent things that could be impacting your thinking positively or negatively. You might be surprised at how many factors are influencing your thoughts.

The Infamous Nature vs. Nurture Argument

Some people wonder if this question will ever be answered because it is fairly similar to the chicken versus the egg at first glance. First and foremost, thoughts originate in biology, and I'm sure you understand why now. The brain is a biological organ that is highly susceptible to change, but it comes before the environment. We are born with a brain that is filled with neurons firing in multiple directions. Therefore, genetics can never be underestimated. Let me present both arguments to you so that you can find clarity.

We like to allocate percentages to both environmental and biological factors in psychology as a general rule. These percentages vary, and I'll give you a breakdown of them. Intelligence is often allocated a genetic portion of 70%, and the remaining 30% can be credited to the environment as one example. Many psychologists believe that environment and biology work hand-in-hand to develop our minds to be what they are today. The fact that the environment plays a role is undeniable, but your brain and the genetic code within are already there. The environment, which can consist of anything external, influences your brain, and the neural network shapes and molds to this stimulus.

Don't misunderstand me either. Yes, biology is the underlying factor, but our environment regulates the biophysical aspect of our brains. You've learned how our neurons, or nerve cells, cycle every two months and how their receptors become attracted to new guidance from the external world. Let's look at a child whose brain is freshly impressionable. The parenting style that a child's parents choose depicts the kid's outcome. I don't disagree with this. A child who grows up in a negligent home is prone to insecurities in their adult life. That strengthens the argument of nurture.

However, think of an inanimate object for a moment. A stone is a non-biological object, and when you mistreat it, the non-existent genetics can't possibly change. This stone cannot become an insecure being because it isn't a living thing. Now take an animal, for example, specifically a mammal who has the closest genetic strands to us. A monkey that is ill-treated will behave inappropriately because their biology in the brain is forming to create negative thoughts.

The bottom line is that the environment cannot have an impact on us without our gray matter shifting and changing to adapt to our surroundings. There is an interesting study that I want to share with you. Kittens were used; they are biological beings who have brains, no matter the size of their brain. They are also mammals that are biologically similar to us.

A study was conducted to examine the critical postnatal period in kittens and regulating their genetics through environmental influence. The first batch of kittens was kept in the dark and developed learned blindness. The second batch of 58 kittens was introduced to the world with goggles. Each pair of goggles either displayed vertical or horizontal lines. When the study was completed, the kittens who experienced vertical lines were blind to horizontal lines, and those exposed to horizontal lines were blind to vertical lines. Imaging was taken from each kitten, and there were visible changes to the part of their brain that receives visuals from their retina (Tanaka et al., 2009). The kittens were protected by local animal cruelty organizations, and the experiment was allowed, just to put your mind at ease.

The purpose of sharing this examination with you is so that you can see this question has no relation to the chicken and the egg debate after all. Our brain circuitry is determined by our external influences, but it all begins in the biological brain activity.

External Influence

Let's take a closer look at how the environment impacts human brains to expand your knowledge. The San Francisco State University conducted a study on people to further solidify the existence of control from external sources (San Francisco State University, 2015). They achieved their suspected result and more when they learned that our consciousness can be influenced without us being aware of it. This only proves that our brain's processes are so fast that we often misunderstand them.

Anyway, 52 participants were exposed to black and white images linked to familiar words that varied in length. Some of these images were of a fox, bicycle, and a heart. The participants were asked not to verbalize the words in their mind or the length of these words. Their automatic responses were to do what they were asked not to. A total of 73% of them verbalized the words internally, and the others counted the number of letters in each. This experiment triggered two different thoughts that were unintentional and confirmed that we don't think consciously.

Our subconscious is in control and reacts swiftly to an external source, whether we're instructed to do so or not. These people were asked not to do what they did, but the thought was planted in their minds when they heard the directives. The instructions were subconsciously processed, and participants were unintentionally influenced to process thoughts. This also helps us understand the difficulty we face in controlling thoughts because they happen automatically and are beyond our control even when we try to diminish them.

Professor of Psychology Ezequiel Morsella explains that we shouldn't see this as a total loss. It can be advantageous in some scenarios when the mind automatically blocks out unwanted thoughts. This study has helped him understand uncontrollable and repetitive thoughts. We have learned that the brain is highly adaptable with practice, and it is part of our evolution.

What can alter our thoughts and embed automatic thoughts? There are numerous external contributors, and I'll run through a few with you. The moment we're confronted with any situation, big or small, our minds see a divided pathway. This intersection can lead down countless roads, but the decision for which road lies within a few factors.

Your past experiences play a major role because they determine how you see the world, yourself, and others. They have shaped your neurons into a form or pattern over time. You understand that this isn't something that happens overnight. Confirmation bias is born on the wings of past memories. The way you experienced something determines how you'll expect to perceive it in the present and future. Another persuader of the brain's patterns lies in the difference of opinion you have compared to another person. The next contributor is the way you see yourself. How relevant do you perceive yourself? Now for the final one I'd like to discuss: The level of commitment you have toward the circumstance you're presented will determine your thoughts and decisions as well.

The Ghost of Our Past

All of the contributors in your thought process and problem-solving abilities lie within your roots. This is how nurture comes into the light once more as it forms our biology. Every person who crosses your path and every experience you succeed with or fail is turning the cog in your machine. I'm going to discuss heuristics to explain how our decisions and the thoughts that drive them are rooted in our past. Heuristics is another concept to explain how we come to a swift decision—similar to fast thinking. But it relates to the road we choose when our thoughts are running free. It is, in fact, the method we choose to arrive at our decision. Heuristics are an immense factor in decision making, and we need to make acceptable decisions in business.

If we look at past influences, we can understand that a decision made yesterday will sway our chosen decision for tomorrow. This goes for both good and bad decisions. I'll use John from our previous discussion as an example here. John encountered difficulty in his business yesterday because he saw the bad review on the internet after offering the customer one month's worth of cheeseburgers to make up for the hair in his hamburger patty. This experience automatically releases tiny fragments of memory in John's brain, and now it will determine how John reacts to his customers today and in the future.

The customer added one line to his review that struck John hard. It could lead to both positive and negative outcomes in future decisions. The customer suggested that the owner or manager is required to remove the burger immediately and replace it with another as the first act of correction. This wasn't John's first thought. He went straight into negotiations while leaving the tainted burger on the table. John feels like a failure now because he didn't react appropriately. His idea of appropriateness lies within the customer's comment. Business owners strongly believe that the customer is always right, and this can impact John's future decisions. We try our best to avoid past mistakes from the information our brain gathers.

Confirmation bias is another derivative of our past. Let's retrace John's original response in the restaurant yesterday. John grew up in a home where he was shown no value or worth and is a highly insecure individual. His father constantly told him that he could never be anything. John approaches the table in an automatic mousey stature, and the customer sees his vulnerability right away. The customer threatens him with a detailed review and gives John no room for negotiation. He finds himself pleading with the client and begs for a solution, looking weaker with every word he voices. John cannot see a solution that will save his restaurant from the inevitable disaster, and the client is permeating with cockiness. Let me tell you a secret before we move on. Yes, the customer is who allows your business to thrive, but there's a balance required between friendliness and respectful assertiveness.

It becomes easier for us to dismiss any additional information because we have all these distorted fragments entering our minds, telling us who we are and what our relevance is. We rely on an accumulation of past experiences to define ourselves, and there can't be another outcome. We find comfort in familiarity. This is where John is stuck in this scenario.

The next scenario is the commitment that John is latched on to. He might have a friend who had a similar incident in their restaurant, and it wasn't a month before they closed their doors for good. This is John's life and livelihood. He sees all his investment in this business and can even carry an unhealthy attachment to it. His fear can escalate horrendously because he automatically assumes that the end is near. What will he do if he loses his business? How can he afford his home and look after his children? There is nothing wrong with being committed to a thought process, but there's a fine line between irrational and logical. John's thoughts and decisions are driven by the depth of which he is "in the hole of commitment."

Factors such as age and gender can play a role too. You have grown up with the belief that older people are more knowledgeable. John is a man in his 40s, and the customer complaining is an adolescent. This could cause John to disregard the opinion of his customer. On the other hand, let's make John a learned sexist. The client is a young female, and he has these deeply engraved biased notions about women having no valid opinions. Keep in mind that these are all examples of clients I've dealt with in my practice, and the distorted notions are not my own. The same could apply to someone who presents themselves as uneducated and unsophisticated. Never judge a book by its cover. The person's appearance could sway John's responsive judgment.

The final external influence I'd like to discuss is one that aligns with common distortions. John could be a man with an overly inflated ego and believes that the ground beneath him is paved with gold. These beliefs hail from assorted past experiences where John has accumulated an arrogant image of himself. It's not only based on the fact that John could be an arrogant man, but it can also stem from his core beliefs. He watches others in business, or perhaps his father owned the restaurant before he took over. His father had used a certain technique in the business, and it's the only one John believes in now. There is no wrong in anything he does. This describes someone who is unintentionally arrogant or what we love to call a "know-it-all."

A Chain Reaction

All the above-mentioned influencers create a chain reaction in our minds. They are responsible for piecing together the fragments from our memory that leads to our initial thoughts. This thinking process is what tells us which road to choose, and then we take action on the said road. Let's run through the examples briefly in action now. I'll use the heuristic, or decision, shortcuts to give you an idea of a bad response that happens when we speak before we think. The actions John takes now will create a boomerang effect and bounce right back into his thoughts, creating new distortions. Every action has a reaction in this life, and in the next, as some people believe.

John has chosen to reply to the review. He chooses to ignore the suggestion of removing the contaminated burger immediately and focuses on an attack to defend his business. This will only backfire because readers will see John reflecting a backlash, and ultimately, the business will diminish. The client can also go into a further attack because they'll raise their defensive walls now in retaliation again. This is going to create a war between them, which will make John feel worse, and his thoughts will distort further.

John became vulnerable in the second example, which opens him up to a thrashing from the client. There's an abuse of his vulnerability instead of mutual respect, and John is overwhelmed with disappointment. John's vulnerability could even be because he doesn't see another answer. He has fallen into the trap of doomed outcome perception. He only sees himself closing the doors and automatically locks out additional information.

John can blow his reputation in the individual variances examples. He looks down at a young man and dismisses any complaints because what does this man know. He is a business owner, and this man knows nothing about food or service quality. He is a spring chicken who needs to grow up. All John did here was hurt his business for future clients.

The final response could be when John refuses to compromise his own beliefs because he knows best. His father taught him how to deal with an unhappy customer, but he forgets about the modern-day millennials.

Any of these negative responses will allow the action to revert to John. The day he closes his doors for the final time is the day he will embed a new distortion in his mind. Everything he has seen and done, including the actions he has taken, will backfire. The same applies to the good decisions he made. It's easy for his head to expand erratically and think too highly of himself if he managed to save the situation miraculously. John is either filled with regret or satisfaction in the completion of his decision, either of which could influence every decision he makes in the future. Humans learn through listening and seeing. When we see an action take place, it will set in motion our perceptions and expectations for a repetition of the previous result.

Cognitive Distortions

Cognitive distortions are the result of all the previously mentioned contributors accumulating and functioning uninterrupted. It can also be defined as someone who has a fault in their thought processes. These will add momentous speed to the thinking process in return, and once a distortion is born, it can grossly exaggerate any future processes. Let's have a look at the common faults in people's processes.

Black and White Tones

This describes someone who fails to see the happy medium, and there is only one option or the other. There is no maybe, and one can do it wrongly or rightly.

Personalization

This is when someone takes everything personally. They blame themselves for any mistakes and doubt their knowledge and methodology.

Should I, or Shouldn't I?

The words should, ought, and must are culprits here. This person will ask themselves if they should've called. They could also believe that someone ought to comply with their expectations. We cannot rely on anyone but ourselves, and this person places unrealistic expectations and doubts in themselves and others.

Warning: Catastrophe Ahead!

This describes someone who catastrophizes something to the extreme. John sees this incident as the absolute end of his business. There is no way he can recover from it. Assuming the worst outcome before it happens is called catastrophizing.

Minimization

John finds himself minimizing his achievements when he downplays the award hanging on the wall. His food is still substandard in his mind, even after his establishment won the local takeout award for the best burgers in town.

Maximizing

I know this sounds similar to the first distortion, but this describes somewhat arrogant people. The business world of entrepreneurship has quite a few of them, just as any industry does. This person will magnify any achievement or event that happened in their business and blow it out of proportion. Their minds tell them that their menial achievement is of great magnitude.

The Mind Reader

This defines someone who has become the local psychic and can tell you exactly what you're thinking and feeling at any given moment. It's a gift they have, and their assumptions are always spot on.

The Fortune Teller

This is the person who knows what the future holds and can't be convinced otherwise. These people often lean to the negative side of outcomes.

The Generalization Expert

This person makes conclusions based on one or two incidents alone and doesn't look at the bigger picture.

The Label Applicator

This is when someone places labels on people and doesn't see past the one mistake they made. It's an inflated version of overgeneralization toward other people.

The Discount Sale

This describes someone who places themselves on sale or at a discounted price. Their negativity dismisses all possible positive attributes, and nothing they do is right.

The Faulty Filtration System

This is someone who will filter through the information until they find one piece of criticism to focus on.

Playing the Blame Game

This person will see no fault in their ways and finds someone else to blame for failure. They infamously pass the buck at every corner.

Reasoning with the Unreasonable

This person sees all emotions as reasonable, and if they feel scared, there must be a viable threat to them.

The Know-It-All

These people believe that everything that comes from their thought processes is the only truth. It doesn't matter how they make people feel, and they refuse to look at someone else's point of view.

Personal Bias

This person takes credit for anything positive and has no clue how the negative could possibly relate to them.

The Fallacy of Heaven's Reward

This is someone who acts compassionately and expects a reward for their long-term selflessness. This distortion becomes dangerous when the reward never surfaces.

The Changing Myth

This person expects people to change to suit their perceptions. They want to be the Geppetto who controls Pinocchio.

The Canard of Fairness

This is when someone thinks the world is fair and that all actions and people will be fair toward them. The world has become a complicated space where fairness doesn't exist.

Controlled Delusion

This person sadly believes that things are out of their control, unavoidably. Every bad experience they have is controlled by some higher being, and they can't change it.

It doesn't matter which of these take hold of someone, they are all serious faults in our circuitry, and no one is exempt from them. The core beliefs that derive from your past can easily deter your path into these distortions.

Cognitive Behavioral Therapy

I've mentioned CBT once before, but allow me to explain what this form of psychology aims to do for you. It's a technique that can be self-applied, and it allows us to deal with the above-mentioned mind issues through evaluation, challenge, alteration, and re-evaluation. Cognitive Behavioral therapy is the amalgamation of two powerful techniques, cognitive psychology and behavioral therapy.

The two treatment options combined when the first became a popular choice for treating a multitude of psychological disorders in its early years. It was used to experiment on anxiety and depression and proved wildly successful. Both of these conditions are the result of faulty thinking patterns. However, it became more than just a psychological tool, and over the years, it was used for pain management and even insomnia. It has worked for conditions beyond the standard psychological spectrums we think we know. You must know that choosing this technique of recovery doesn't label someone as insane. If I've taught you anything up to this point, it's that the problem is biological, and external sources regulate the current. This doesn't mean that you were born with a mental condition. We are all susceptible to life and all it throws at us.

Nevertheless, this method of "talk therapy," as called by many psychologists, provides you with the tools you need to achieve multiple benefits yourself. It even includes slow-thinking exercises. Frequently, we need the strength in proven techniques to help us over the slump in our lives. Cognitive behavior therapy will identify problematic thoughts or cognitions about yourself, others, and the world around you. It will pinpoint the beliefs and memories that drive you to have any possible distortion and acknowledge the responses that come from them. Some activities allow you to see things rationally and delegate various outcomes. You have to scan every corner of your universal globe to find the pixels that hinder your harmony. It takes into account the predisposing factors and perpetuating aspects. It even looks into lifestyle habits that might be maintaining a certain distortion. These thoughts will be brought to the surface and challenged with new thinking patterns.

The point is that you cannot solve a problem if you don't acknowledge it, and CBT enlightens you to any thoughts that impact your feelings and behavior. That's why self-evaluation is key. You will place your cognitions and every reactive cycle under scrutiny and adjust them with alternative solutions. This form of therapy, or "self-therapy," will help you to recognize any problems that are contributing to your shortfalls. This includes your diet, sleep patterns, relationships, and even financial stability. New information will present itself when you allow vital thinking time and assess the day on paper.

You'll be guided to new heights when you align yourself with goals that are well within your reach and attaining the skill set required to reach them. You will stabilize your activity and reduce any experiences that push a faulty network over the edge. It's imperative to circumvent any self-damaging thoughts and the beliefs that caused them to be there. It isn't necessary to live with these problems. Every time you think about inevitable failure without reasonable evidence thereof, your mind has wandered dangerously into the field of dysfunctional cognitions again.

There will be a reward for your progress, and you'll measure each step you take. Rewards are used to positively reinforce alternative behaviors and thoughts so that your brain chemistry can latch onto a new habit. So please do reward yourself accordingly. You want new cells to grow and contain the receptors needed for a wholesome and successful life. The new emotions that accompany substituted thoughts will encourage your brain to want to return to the introductory feeling. Yes, even your neurons are prone to temptation.

Cognitive behavioral therapy targets the connection between thoughts, behavior, and emotions that lead to a specific and sometimes undesired response. It will help you raise yourself from the negative schema that surrounds you. Let's face it, cognitive distortions are strongly related to negative thinking. Any business owner will understand the devastating consequences of negativity. Rise from the ashes and take the lead in your career. CBT will allow you to do just that. I'll provide some introductory exercises in Chapter 6.

Chapter 5:

The Simplest Guide to

Controlling Your Thought

Process

You know that consciousness and subconscious processes impact the function of the mind. You've been introduced to the valuable slow-thinking method, but now you need the tools to apply it. This chapter will pinpoint the actual steps and strategies that will allow you to slow down and exercise better control over any potentially destructive thought processes.

Can Thoughts Be Controlled?

Your mind is made up of the conscious and subconscious minds you've learned about, and the first is the slow-moving process, whereas the second is the fast jolt of electricity that runs through your neural system. Conscious awareness lies at the beginning and the end of the task at hand. You know what needs to be done to start, and you have an idea of the result needed. This indicates that conscious thoughts, the ones we have a vast power to control, are merely a fraction of the entire administration.

Underneath the layer of easily controlled thoughts lies a level of subconsciously deeper thoughts. You've learned much about these patterns and the superhighways they travel on. The speeds alone can be intimidating as the functions automatically take over. Let me give you an example to differentiate the two layers. I'll use one that relates to the speeds in more than one way.

A Formula One race car driver is sitting at the start line and thinking about winning the race. He ponders all possibilities while he listens to the engines revving beside him. He feels this monstrous horse-powered machine beneath him, vibrating through his body. He can see the finish line in his mind and feels the cold metal gear shift under his hand. His conscious thoughts are riling him up, and he is excitedly waiting for the lights to begin the race. He runs all thoughts through his mind one last time.

He is sitting in the far left grid at the start and mentally creates an image of his fragmented memory to remind him of any sharp corners on the circuit. He plans his laps and the weak spots in the circuit that will give him a jump on the competition. He knows how many pit stops he'll have to make before the race is over. He calculates which laps these need to happen in. He knows that the ultimate goal is to race over the finish line, and he feels the desire burning in him to come in no place other than first position. He has a winning mindset.

The first light illuminates, and his attention is drawn to the track ahead of him. His engine is gaining volume and veracity. This is the final moment where his conscious thoughts are in control. As the fifth light radiates, his tires spin rapidly against the tarmac, and he feels the adrenaline rush through his veins as he takes off like a Boeing. His subconscious mind immediately takes action because the conscious mind processes information too slowly. All thought processes are executing their functions now, and they even adapt as he glides into the pit stop two laps earlier than he originally planned. His conscious mind didn't take the distance into account and failed to realize that he needed to refuel earlier than he first planned to. The driver continues to zoom around the circuit and finally reaches the final lap.

He has set his eyes on the target, the same finish line that was the starting line. His conscious mind might take over for a moment again when he directs his attention to the goal in front of him. As he crosses the finish line, his mind slows down, and the autopilot is disengaged.

Your subconscious must take control in a situation where you need to think swiftly, and it will adapt to needed changes. The power this driver exerted over his thought process was by directing his attention to the task at hand. His single goal was to race over the finish line. He spent time focusing on the specifics before he sped off. The overall task was to reach the finish line, but he spent time thinking slowly about the pit stops and the corners he needed to cut that wouldn't damage his tires.

The moral of this example is that thoughts don't just pop into our minds for no reason. There are countless precursors that drive the process. These are the thoughts that need to be controlled in a slow-thinking fashion to achieve what might seem impossible at first. The driver in this example understands what needs to be done because this is his career, and he's been racing for years. Although, it's not necessary to know every aspect of the task before you tackle it; you just have to slow down and consider all options.

Think through each possibility logically and feel free to welcome any new knowledge or advice. If you wish to host a conference for the first time, do some research and speak to people who know what to do and expect. You can expose your mind to the contributors you need to think about before your automatic subconscious Boeing completes the task. So yes, the answer to the question is that you can modify and control your subconscious thoughts successfully through manipulating your conscious thoughts.

Primary Techniques to Rectify Thought Cycles

I want you to mindfully envision what I explain in this section to benefit from the full advantage. There are two primary techniques for controlling your thoughts, but we need to give these cognitions a face first. I assume that you are in business, so I will use a business visualization to explain the encompasses of your thoughts. You have started a new company and are the chief executive officer (CEO) of all operations. This company's name is Self. You must understand who's in charge because you are, and no one else can be. However, you have employees in your company, and I'll give each one of them a name and personality of their own.

Imagine yourself sitting in the boardroom of your new company. You have four major executives sitting around the table with you, and they help you make decisions that appear to be justified for the company.

The first seemingly executive employee is called *the doubter,* and he is your worst critic, to say the least. Every decision placed on the table is broken down by him, and he wants to remind you of everything other people have said to you before, including your parents. He will bring to the light any thoughts you've previously delved into about the expectations of your company.

These are from yourself and others. *The doubter* loves to compare you to other people, often irrelevant or incomparable people in the media. He has the memory of an elephant and points out any traumatic memories that made you feel worthless or to blame for something, even if this pain was caused by rejection or betrayal that was out of your control. This devious character thrives on pain, low self-esteem, and blocks you from loving or accepting yourself. *The doubter* undoubtedly abuses you—pun intended. Take a moment to remember who this is because all these board members are a vital part of your Self company.

The next executive is called *the anxious seer.* This monstrosity of an executive can magically see into the future and will undeniably pinpoint any possible shortfalls the company of Self can succumb to. He finds motivation in fear and makes irrational suggestions with no grounds to support it. He also loves reminding you of past fears and will try everything to convince you of their validity.

The third board member is called *the Fukushima reactor*. This nuclear reactor is driven by nothing but a loss of impulse control. He explodes at ideas drawn on the board and brings up past mistakes and memories to erupt with anger, pain, and frustration. Any thought considered that resembles a past wound in any shape or form will allow this famous reactor to melt down.

The fourth executive that sits in the boardroom is called *the Freddy Kruger puppeteer*. This member has a group of administrators himself who is always uninvitedly present. They include *the reiterator*, *the ruminator*, and the *inconspicuous inner planner*, among others. He influences the company and often keeps the meeting going on beyond business hours. You can call him the nightmare of your waking dreams, and he loves to deprive you of sleep. He controls *the doubter* and *the anxious seer* as well. His motivation is driven by silence when he seeks a reaction. He is also responsible for keeping you awake in the company of Self until you have finished the day's business, in his opinion. He is a real arrogant donkey. He believes he is the voice of self-doubt, low self-esteem, anxiety, and insecurities. The moment your Self company wishes to rest at night, he is there, instigating trouble.

Now you've set the scene of your business or "mind" on any given day, and we can use the two primary techniques to put these employees in their place.

Technique A teaches you to interrupt their intermissions in your meetings and replace them with others. Technique B is known to eliminate harmful staff. Different executives will require different techniques. Take a seat at the head of the boardroom table and listen to my instructions.

Technique A allows you to interrupt *the doubter* and *the anxious seer*. These people who sit around the company table of Self are fragments of your subconscious mind. They are you, and you will interject their disruptions by forcefully presenting new ideas to them. They will resist at first, but you can continue to present these new alternatives until they latch onto them like a leach in a swamp. These two executives are highly impressionable, and you can coax them into redirection in the future by reprogramming their "minds."

Let's look at *the doubter* individually. Every time he speaks up in a meeting, you should express your authority. When he tells you that you can't do something or belittles you in *your* company, use your inner voice to assertively tell him to shut up. Make it known that you're in control, and this company belongs to you. The next time he tells you that you're a disappointment and can't succeed in the industry you've chosen, tell him that you are a capable human who continues to grow every day. You can even say this out loud if you must. Speak over him and keep telling him that you are perfect the way you are with every reason he gives to solidify his words. Create an inner dialog where you present alternatives. Put him under the spotlight and tell him that it doesn't matter if someone said you can't succeed because they're one droplet in the ocean of people.

Make a list of affirmations that relate to you individually and the critical doubt he mentions frequently. Prepare yourself for his next attack. The problem is that he stirs *the anxious seer* and the horrible names he calls you to become embedded, causing *the Fukushima reactor* to step in. He will even encourage *the Freddy Kruger puppeteer* to keep you awake at night. You can hire and fire employees, and if he won't listen to your demands, kick him out. You can replace him with an executive driven by your compassionate, supportive, and life-enhancing affirmations. There are no unions in your mind, after all. I advise you to write your affirmations down and repeat them to yourself three times a day, every day.

The anxious seer can be felt in your partner company of "body" when he activates. I want you to disrupt his inconceivable control in your company by writing a list of things you're grateful for. Repeat these grateful verbalizations daily as you do with the affirmations because if he isn't prepared to change his attitude in the company, you can replace him with a new employee. Threaten him by forcefully repeating words when you feel your heartbeat speed up or you see specks in front of your eyes because your blood pressure is rising. He believes he is the predictor of the future, and your gratitude verbalization will positively "predict an alternative future." He will say, "I'm afraid of the meeting with our new client tomorrow because of this and that, which happened 10 years ago." You will speak over him confidently and say, "I am grateful for the opportunity arriving tomorrow because the client would like to see my company portfolio. They must have heard great things, and I'm thankful for the person who spoke of those things." Smile as you say this because a smile exerts confidence.

The Fukushima reactor is a sensitive matter and needs the right approach. This man needs to be mentally eliminated from your meeting altogether. You will react physically to him when he speaks up and focus your attention on your breathing. Count to 10 slowly while you breathe in gently through your nose and feel the air fill your lungs. You can see your stomach and chest rise as you hold the breath for a second before you follow it out through your mouth. Empty your lungs with every exhale and try to maintain one breath per count until you reach 10. You can continue this for another count of 10 until you face the reactor with a calm face and show your dominance. You don't want this guy to explode and activate *the Freddy Kruger puppeteer.*

Now we come to the guy who believes that the company of Self belongs to him. You want to fire this "sleep depriver" and kick out all his supportive cronies. The moment *the Freddy Kruger puppeteer* raises his voice, you begin your calming breathing exercise again. Pay close attention to the rise and fall of your chest. This executive will try to raise his voice further and instigate every other employee to join him. Block his ruminating speech with an additional focus while breathing. Direct your attention to the word "in" as you inhale and elongate it so that it lasts through the entire intake. Change the word to "out" when you exhale and focus hard on the words themselves. Use your inner voice to increase the volume of these words with each cycle, drowning out the volume from *the Freddy Kruger puppeteer.*

You are forcing your brain to slow down, and the subconscious mind becomes aware of the slow dialog forming. All the executives around your boardroom table are continuing to speak over each other, but you can feel the chaos distancing itself from your CEO seat. You are taking control by slowing down and distancing the shouting around the table. Don't be surprised if your mind becomes calm enough to drift off when you revoke the power from *the Freddy Kruger puppeteer* and reinstate it in yourself.

Both techniques require practice and won't shift the balance overnight. Don't give up, but continue these strategies to eliminate the influence of these possessive employees.

Acknowledgment and Acceptance

Robin Sharma once said, "Everything is created twice. First in the mind and then in reality." It's time to make peace with your mind and methods inspired by CBT therapy, and mindfulness will teach you to do just that. There's no doubt that invasive and persistent thoughts will always have a role in your existence, but they don't need to define you. You can never remove the fast, emotional responses entirely, but you can minimize them exponentially. It matters that you understand your thoughts because then, you'll see that they're just that and no more. They don't need to govern your actions. Observing your mind will expose the patterns of how these thoughts came into existence. You need to regain conscious power and stop trying to regulate subconscious thoughts that move at speeds somewhat inconceivable. This is what I will focus on in this section.

To become the only CEO of your company again, you can follow this simple step-by-step practice daily as one option.

The first step is when you listen and acknowledge the projections of subconscious beings in your boardroom. Think of these interrupters as disgruntled employees and calm the chaos by listening intently to what they have to say. Show them that you are all ears. Offer gratitude for their opinion. Their tamed chaos will now express a more understandable message. I know these employees can drive you insane at times, but sometimes, their message will indirectly enlighten you on an area that needs work. *The anxious seer* might be speaking of a meeting tomorrow morning that will be the end or a new beginning for your business, and his opinion isn't always unreasonable because it directs your focus to the expected meeting, and you can work on perfecting your presentation.

Secondly, make peace through negotiations with these parties in your mind. You know it isn't helping you when there's a constant shouting match across the table. Yes, you've learned to breathe, but if you see these executives as potentially valuable assets, you need to negotiate with them. Listening and acknowledging them has already set the ball rolling on compromise and peaceful negotiations. Discuss your goals with your employees and allow them the opportunity to respond. You don't have to accept every aspect of their response, but you can open the floor for debate so that the previously warring parties can all feel some level of importance below you.

The third vital step is seeing these employees for what they are. Thoughts are physical, yes, but each of these employees is part of the bigger picture. *The doubter* may mention a point, but his opinion is based on underlying factors. Delve into those factors and question the reason why he feels you are worthless. The influence external contributors have on this thoughtful participant form a habit, and habits can be good or bad. He is just projecting a habit that has been in your fragmented memories for a long time. It will take time to change the habits within this projection of thoughts.

The fourth step is learning to know your enemy. Al Pacino is a famous American actor who often quotes, "Keep your friends close and your enemies closer." The quote originated from the brilliant military strategist in the Chinese army called Sun Tzu (545 to 470 B.C.). You cannot expect to learn every weakness and strength of an opponent without getting to know them. These executives are currently your enemy, and you need to learn every point of interest surrounding them. Mindfulness will help you do this because you need a way to observe the actions, reactions, and thoughts of each employee in your company. This can help you identify problems before they reach their boiling point.

The next step is to rewire your brain through staff training. Jim Rohn once said, "Success is nothing more than a few simple disciplines, practiced daily." Notice how we master a skill physically when we practice it for a long time. It's even true when a child learns to read and write. The same applies to thoughts because we've learned how we can encourage the growth of new neurons and receptors. Practice new thoughts every day without fail and watch as the executives around your table grasp them gradually. You are training your employees because you want the business to run smoother than it did before. Provide them with product knowledge as well. When *the Fukushima reactor's* face turns red, provide him with evidence as to why he shouldn't be angry. Sit him down and gather new possible factors. Maybe the client didn't return your call today because they were caught up in an emergency? Their failure to call doesn't mean they chose an opposition company. Life happens to everyone, and life might have handed the client lemons. Give it time.

The final step in reprogramming your company's function is to learn self-compassion. The doubter will come into play when emotions run amok from past experiences. They will criticize everything that's happening, and you are disappointed in the behavior of this employee. Show some compassion because it can open doors to other ideas. Don't dismiss any sad memories that he speaks of and allow him to share the entire picture. Discuss the memory with him, and you might find that it brings sadness and joy simultaneously. The same experience he mentions was depressing, but it also brought a smile to your face when you bumped into an old friend. Emotions can contain useful information too. They could indicate that you are tired and need rest to carry on. Feelings from *the doubter* or *the anxious seer* could help you take the break you need before you break down.

This is one form of working together with your colleagues or employees once they know who's boss, and it can lead to deserved loyalty from them. This strategy helps when your workers aren't corrupted by *the Freddy Kruger puppeteer*. You know how to handle this monster if he tries to delegate.

Redirection

I want to supply you with a few more tips to practice in your company of Self. This is another collection of advice that requires practice, and the longer you continue with these visuals and inner dialog, the deeper your influence will permeate. The CEO is the one person who has a vision for the company, after all, and that's you. Don't expect employees to have the same vision as you do.

The first one involves you deciding how you want to feel. Are you happy with the feelings that regulate your mind daily? You've opened observation in the previous section, and now it's time to choose your desired feelings and create a new state of mind. Move the attention away from negative emotions and focus on positive alternatives. Do you like feeling angry? No, I'm sure you don't, and you can make a conscious decision right now to feel optimistic and happy. Use role-play to introduce your company to new emotions. Delve into the details of how contentment feels.

See yourself as a Buddhist monk who has disciplined themselves to avoid distraction from what they desire. Close your eyes and walk through a day in this new CEO's life. Begin in the morning and see how this person wakes up with a smile on their face. Watch as they calmly turn the radio up when they're stuck in traffic. Visualize them in the workplace and how they react appropriately to stressors. Decide how they switch off after a long day at the office. You are the director of this role-play, and all aspects must remain positive. Live in that fantasy world for a moment because that's how you introduce new habits to your workers. They are seeing what you imagine and feel the way you do at that moment.

The next part of your new daily routine will include brief groundwork for 10 minutes each day, when you re-enter this imaginative state. This helps you remind yourself of the burning desire that you've created in the first place. Focus on your breathing and the sensations it brings to your body. Close your eyes and center yourself in the present to repeat the image of who you want to be. Suppress all negative self-talk and rehearse your successes of the day. It doesn't matter how menial they might seem, but you will credit yourself for every achievement, big and small. You accomplished a great feat today when you diffuse a bomb between an employee and a client.

Build a powerful toolkit from what you've seen in the Self company. What does it need to function properly?

Is your first vision suitable, or should you alter it? Every mind and every boardroom of the mind's company needs a different approach. Focus on your motivations and challenges. Your challenge might be negativity, and I have a solution for this. Keep in mind that my solution might not work for you. You will find a unique routine for yourself, but you're welcome to try mine to start.

You're going to force positivity into your company with physical actions. Smile to instruct your brain that happy time has arrived. Then you can wiggle your legs because any spontaneous movement will help relieve tension in your muscles. Verbally voice an affirmation out loud. It can be something like, "I am successful, and accomplishment lives inside me." Do this a few times. Take a deep breath in and exhale forcefully but slowly to blow all the tension out of your body.

The final advice I can give you in this chapter is that change begins with you. You can't expect someone else to shift the direction of your flow, and once you move your mind from negative to positive, the results will come gradually.

Chapter 6:

The Body-Mind Connection: Why Thinking Time is Even More Important Than You Initially Believed

Some of the previous chapters have already highlighted the fact that thoughts can impact one's physiological condition. This is known as the mind-body connection and is yet another important reason why slowing down and taking enough time to think happens to be so vital for a more conscious and satisfactory existence.

A Brief Overview of Facts

I want to summarize the connection between your mind and body once more so that you can understand how the two work harmoniously with each other. Nothing has changed, and scientists often debate dualism. Dualism is the idea that our minds and body are two separate entities. This was originally proposed by the 17th-century French philosopher Rene Descartes. Even though the two are separate and operate individually, they also interact with each other constantly. Descartes taught of the pineal gland being the connection point between the two. Not that much was understood about the glands involved yet, and he simply meant the heart of our brain.

I've given you in-depth anatomy of the brain and how each gland or control center speaks to another through the network of neurons that span over the entire system. The hypothalamus communicates with glands across our bodies to produce hormones and chemicals in reaction to stress, fatigue, and various other emotions. Our emotions are responses to the collection of memory pixels that accumulate to instigate thought, and this builds an emotional reaction.

Modern-day psychology continues to investigate the connection between our thoughts, emotions, and the changes in our bodies. Scientists and researchers can follow the link between them by using imaging devices such as MRI and computed tomography (CT) scans. The examination of specific brain states or patterns has directly been linked to many health conditions that hinder our lives.

Robert Ader from the Department of Psychiatry at the University of Rochester Medical Center began a research program called psychoneuroimmunology in the 1970s. Ader was concerned about people's disregard for mental health because he believed that it could sever the connection between the mind and body. We all try our best to maintain healthy bodies, but we neglect our minds, and that's a dangerous mistake (Rackley, 2016).

Psychoneuroimmunology delves into the effects of the nervous system on our immune systems. Stress and anxiety can impact the immune system drastically. You know that stress causes the neural network to instruct the release of cortisol, and the effects of this alone can be devastating. Excessive amounts of cortisol can assist the shut down of our immune system when it mimics proteins in our body, and then our bodies become fragile to externally and internally harmful sources. Your body can even become resistant to cortisol. The immune system contains chemicals called lymphocytes that kill off alien bacteria. Cortisol suppresses these agents in your blood. This makes us vulnerable to disease and infection when our immune system takes a prolonged break.

The best way you can avoid this disconnection in the two entities is to see and treat them as one. The mind and body cannot work as individual enterprises without assistance from the other.

Neuroscientist Antonio Domasio is often expressing his thoughts on the matter. He asks a simple question that helps us understand the connection better. How does the environment impact our neural activity if not through the brain? Yes, the external world can be seen through our eyes, and the event that happens in front of us triggers thought processing. What about the touch of your skin against a silky texture? This begins with your hands, and the sensation is perceived and evaluated by your brain. We can assume the same when we link the connection of internal influences. You have thought about your mom who passed away three months ago, and suddenly, you feel a physical strain over your heart. This response has been triggered by your thoughts, but it doesn't end there because your increased heart rate triggers the release of cortisol.

I will refer back to my description of the brain as a universe of its own. Many scientists would love to upload our brains to an artificial intelligence source. However, this is complicated for two reasons. The brain requires the body to function in its current capacity. People who've undergone heart transplant surgeries have attempted to convince us that they carry the memories and new personalities of the donor. This isn't entirely true though. They can't possibly contain the physical memories that were fragmented in the brain of another person. They can, however, see changes in their personalities.

The reason this happens is pragmatic. The person suffered from physical ailments that led to them needing a new heart. A failing heart causes pain and physical symptoms that impact our thought processes. It's easy to feel "off" when we have thoughts of death looming near, and when our hearts are renewed physically, these thoughts shift to optimistic compasses.

The second problem with artificial intelligence is the complexity of our "universe," or brain. Science doesn't understand enough about the brain to perfectly map out every neuron and its synapses. Technology hasn't reached that stage yet. How can we transfer a consciousness in its entirety, along with its subconsciousness, without fully understanding every aspect of it? We have made great strides in organ transplants in the body, but the brain itself is misunderstood, and it can't function without the body. How is a machine going to correlate senses to specific regions in the brain to stimulate thoughts if the body doesn't exist? This sadly disproves the famous baseball player Ted Williams' idea to have his brain frozen after death. He saw his brain as a single entity. You cannot recreate a person with the exact replication of genetics if the body is gone.

We can almost return to our discussion of the soul for this part. I would rename it the personality in this case. Yes, I agree that the "soul," or personality, resides in the brain, but without its influence and partnership from the body, it can never be the same entity it was before. Your current body and brain are what make you the person you are today.

There's another interesting field of research that has intrigued me called transhumanism. This is the idea of connecting our brains to the vast world of online information through a brain implant. The idea of a chip in my brain that allows me to connect to the internet without speaking or typing might be interesting to some, but the brain is far too complex to attach a physical object to it. Where do we begin? Do we connect it to the prefrontal cortex where memories are stored temporarily or permanently? Is it possible to store memories permanently without the influence of our senses? How do the strands of information attach themselves to our receptors if there's no connection to touch, sight, smell, hearing, and taste? You cannot taste an object with the brain itself. The sensors on your tongue are what creates the connection.

There is an endless amount of information available to us to expand on the fact that our mind and body are interconnected on every level, and it will help you understand the need for the physical exercises I'll introduce as well.

The Consequences of Thoughts on Our Health

I've spoken of endorphins in the first chapter, but they genuinely deserve recognition for what they are. Your brain releases endorphins when you feel content, excited, motivated, and accomplished. Yes, they make you feel better than you already do, but they can also act as a natural painkiller. This, along with a chemical called gamma globulin, has the opposite effect of excessive cortisol in your body. These are two chemicals responsible for strengthening your immune system.

You should never underestimate the power of your thoughts again because being an optimistic person can work wonders for you. An article was published in the *American Journal of Lifestyle Medicine* in 2016 that might sway your outlook on life (Park et al., 2016). Optimism is the way to go according to science and psychology. Teaching individuals to be positive has had great benefits in their overall health. It decreases their recovery time from ailments, and they don't fall ill as often anymore. Their resilience toward disease is higher, and their immune systems are ready for any battle that may present itself. Positive people face a shortened healing time for wounds, and it's even suppressed the symptoms of chronic disorders.

This is another form of tricking our brains in some way because when you keep telling yourself that you will get better, your brain releases chemicals that boost your immune system and voila, you recover faster. It's some form of the placebo effect that we discussed before.

Negative thoughts are detrimental over long periods. It prevents the production of these immune-boosting chemicals, and your body struggles to heal. There is a dangerous game of roulette that takes place when your hormones and chemicals become unbalanced. Stress is one of the instigators of acute inflammation, and this leads to chronic inflammation. The immune system goes into attack mode when it perceives a threat to any part of your neural system and releases cytokines in response to build inflammation. Inflammation is the immune system's automatic response to injury and infection. You can see negative thoughts like an infection in disguise.

Chronic inflammation can lead to life-changing conditions such as diabetes, high blood pressure, cancer, and heart disease, to name a few. A persistent case of inflammation can irritate the blood vessels in your body and cause a build-up of plaque. This plaque can break loose, or blood clots can form in your constricted bloodstream that can even lead to a major stroke. A stroke affects the brain on so many levels because if there's a lack of oxygen flowing to one region of the brain, the cells in that area can die before they procreate.

Negative thoughts have an immense reaction in our bodies. The longer we walk side-by-side, the harder it is to let go. Your body goes into a constant fight-or-flight mode when you are persistently worried and fearful. It is only a matter of time before you see the physical consequences of remaining in this rumination mindset. Negative schema is a medical condition and should be taken seriously. There will always be hope for you to emerge victorious because of the two-month cycle that exists in your nerve cells.

Strengthening the Mind-Body Connection

The moment you understand the connection between the mind and body, which is complicated beyond words, is the moment you begin your journey to self-healing. Some exercises have proven beneficial to strengthening the connection, and I've briefly introduced them throughout the book. I've met many people who come across as the strongest minds I've encountered. You would never believe the problems that lie beneath the surface. The only difference is that they've learned to control these issues in their psychological biology.

I'm going to spend a few moments giving you a simple CBT psychology exercise so that you can set your goals and acknowledge what needs alteration. It all begins with awareness. You are going to study your thought processes, recognize your triggers (or negative influences), and use alternatives to overcome them. Rewiring your brain will supply you with powerful self-healing in your mind and body and realign your reality.

CBT Exercises

The first assignment I want you to complete and implement in your daily life is a thought journal. You can create a spreadsheet in Microsoft Excel to keep updating every day and refer to it when you need to. It will consist of seven columns and an endless amount of rows.

The first column will be where you enter your triggers. Think about the day you had and what triggered a negative thought. Was it when your employee disrespected a client?

The second column will record any emotions you feel at the moment of the trigger or even when you think about it. Give the emotion a percentage of significance. This might include a percentage of 80 for anger.

The third column will contain any thoughts that popped into your mind in the circumstance. You might have thought of dismissing the employee because of their behavior.

The fourth column provides you with facts to support, and the fifth column is facts that are against the thought. Supporting facts can include customer service expected from your employees. Facts against might include the fact that this is a known problematic customer who attempts to return items constantly without a receipt.

The sixth column is where you write down any alternative thoughts or decisions to implement. Your new decision is that the employee should be called in for investigation tomorrow, and you will give them a warning for their behavior. You won't dismiss them because you're well aware that the client is a trouble-maker.

The last column will record your emotions after trying alternative thoughts. Don't forget to jot down your new percentage as well. Anger might reduce to 30% now, and this whole exercise has allowed you to challenge your thoughts and realize how alternative responses can make you feel better.

The second exercise I'll introduce you to is practical. You've spent time visualizing your goals of who you want to be in the previous chapter. Now you can record them on paper or another worksheet.

Welcome the SMART system into your life. The acronym stands for specific, measurable, achievable, relevant, and timeous when describing goals, and it is commonly used in CBT. Think about the person you wish to be. You want to be the lion of your industry to be someone that others look up to.

Let's be specific about it. You are in the hospitality industry. You have one small coffee shop now, and you want to record the exact specifics of what your goal will be. Do you want to franchise your coffee shop in 10 years? Do you want to see your face in the media for being the business person of the year in your town? Make notes of every detail that pertains to your ultimate target.

Now you will create a measurable timeline. How many years or months to reach the goal? Set yourself specific milestones to follow your progress. The next step is ensuring that your goal is achievable. Is it possible for you to reach the goal in the time you've given yourself? Do your skills allow it, or can you add any skills you need? The fourth part of goal setting is deciding whether it is relevant to your industry. Your goal isn't relevant when you wish to be the owner of a hotel franchise if you specialize in coffee shops. The final stage is timeous, and this is the start of your timeline. Are you going to start now or next week?

There you go. These two exercises will boost your mind-body connection when you create awareness and open the door to challenges.

Mindfulness Techniques

Some of the greatest techniques are included in this section. Harnessing power from mindfulness will help you reach the goals you've recorded and give you the strength to be the greatest version of you that has ever existed. You will learn to manage stress so that this villain doesn't decline your wellbeing again. Mindfulness will remove or reduce chronic pain with long-term practice. It will also help you surface any repressed emotions that have manifested themselves in your physical health.

Exercise is necessary to hone these abilities to perfection. They include progressive muscle relaxation, relaxation breathing, yoga, tai chi, and guided imagery meditation. They will further empower your awareness and enable you to control these ANTs in your mind. It is easier to control your body after all because it's not as complicated as your thoughts. That's why I want you to start here. I'll give you a breakdown or a simple example of each.

Tai Chi

This form of mindfulness training can't be verbally taught. Tai Chi is a Chinese form of martial arts that is often used for reasons other than self-defense. It's used to teach participants how to move their bodies in certain gentle movements that relax your muscles and opens your airways. These slow movements have helped people in meditation as well. Sign up at your local dojo or look for instructional videos online.

Yoga

Yoga is another form of physical movement. The instructor will teach you how to move into specific positions that open "chakras" in your system. I would advise an instructor because you don't want to injure yourself. Physically, you can see this form of exercise as one that opens a certain region of your body to relax the muscles and encourage the flow of communications through it. Some positions improve breathing, and others inspire the release of tension in muscles. It enhances your physical health and helps you enter a meditative state as well. Yoga uses breathing, meditation, relaxation, and mindfulness simultaneously in the singular actions of the body and has been practiced for many years, even in the Western world.

Progressive Muscle Relaxation Combined with Breathing Relaxation

I've introduced you to breathing exercises in the previous chapter, but I want you to follow my lead on a combined technique to release the tension in your muscles at the same time. Find a comfortable space to sit and read this the first few times before you learn to grow comfortable with the exercise yourself.

Straighten your back and sit with your legs crossed. Take a deep breath in through the nose and out through the mouth. There's no need to close your eyes. Drop your eyes down to look toward your nose and focus intently on the image below it. Keep breathing deeply and follow the flow of air into your lungs. Hold it before you release it. Continue breathing in and out while you focus on the rise of your chest. Any thought that tries to invade your peaceful space can exit with the breath that leaves your body. Keep your breaths even and listen to your heart as it slows down more with each exhale.

Shift your attention to your feet and feel how heavy they appear. Take a deep breath and hold it as your heart is beating slow but powerfully. Your heart pushes a flood of blood down to your extremities. The oxygenated blood grasps the heaviness in your feet, and the flow of blood comes back to your chest area. Keep breathing evenly as you allow the blood to magnetically pull the tension from your legs back into your chest region. Follow the circulation to your stomach region as the blood pulls the heaviness from the region. You can feel the sensation flow into your chest.

You don't want too much pressure on your heart, so take another deep breath in and feel the pressure latch onto the air in your lungs. Visualize this and feel it with your senses. The fresh air is scooping every ounce of heaviness from your chest area. Now follow the air as it assertively presses through your throat and out of your mouth. It carries the pressure from your muscle tension that accumulated in your chest.

Return to your even breaths and follow the circulation of blood in your body again. The red fluid flows into your hands and grabs the tension in your muscles before it drags it back to your chest. Your breath remains perfectly even as you follow the flow back into your arm to grasp the heaviness that resides there. Your arms feel lighter as the blood pushes tension into the area of your lungs, waiting for its exit. Now the blood flows through your shoulders and into your neck, collecting all the pressure that resides in your muscles before it tugs it back into your exit region. Finally, the blood flows into your brain through all those arteries and ventricles that flow past the neural highways of information. There's a vast amount of tension, and your circulation makes two trips as you continue breathing evenly.

Feel the pressure build in your chest as the heaviness is stored there and awaiting ejection from your body. Take a deep breath and allow the air to fully take over in your lungs before its dispelled. Your entire body falls into an unfamiliar deep state of relaxation as the last of the pressure presses through your lips. This calming relaxation welcomes you, and you welcome it back. It feels euphoric, and there isn't an ounce of tension left in your body. Continue breathing evenly for another count of 20 before you release the state. Focus on the weightlessness of your muscles as you count to 20 slowly and listen to how steady your heart is beating. Your chest is still rising and falling with each inhale and exhale.

Guided Imagery Meditation

Meditation and hypnosis have become vastly popular, and the internet provides us with countless guides on YouTube and Audible. Download a few and follow them. I'm only going to introduce you briefly to one. It will be similar to the visualization in the previous chapter. You are most welcome to practice breathing and muscle relaxation before you enter into a guided image creation. These are best when you close your eyes, but you can keep them open for my sample. I will assume that you relaxed your muscles with the exercise I provided and are now in a deeply calm state of mind. Read my words, but I'd like you to visualize my exercise on your own as soon as you know what to see. This will be a simple acknowledgment of your brain and its systems.

Find yourself in that perfectly relaxed state as you continue to listen to the beats of your heart. Breathe in and out evenly while you follow your blood circulation back into the brain by passing through the brainstem. You can visualize the brainstem as you enter the brain itself. Imagine the image in front of your inner eyes. Your entire being is calm and experiencing slow waves where you can surf them subconsciously.

Look at the amazing network that flows through your brain. You can see the hypothalamus and the pineal gland as your rise above them and into the thalamus. Focus on the electrical pulses running from one gland to another. Move your visual attention to the prefrontal cortex where you can see the process of your mind sorting the fragments of this very memory into little fragments, separating them and sending them into the network. You follow the light as one of them reaches a receptor down the line of communications.

You recognize the memory. It was the time the first thought of entrepreneurship entered your mind. You can feel the emotions that came with the fragment— happiness and excitement beyond your wildest imagination. Allow the flood of emotions to take control of you for a moment. Bathe in the shower of feel-good feelings. You can see a new stream of light shooting up from your interbrain where the pineal gland and hypothalamus reside.

There is a massive attraction entering your emotions now. You cannot remove your inner eyes from the sight that's heading straight toward you. It's a light like no other, and it beckons you closer. The light emits dopamine, and you reach an even deeper state of peace. All worries and fears suddenly leave your presence as the light touches your soul. You can see your team of executive employees surrounding you as the light touches each of you. The doubter has a new expression on his face. It resembles acceptance, and it's the first time you see this person smile.

You look back at the prefrontal cortex and see thousands of new fragments entering the system. You want to remain here forever because it's a feeling you have never known, but the only way to keep it is to exit the brain again. Take slightly deeper breaths now and feel yourself travel back with every beat of your heart. Allow your imagination to slip away from your grasp until you reach the 10th breath. Your consciousness returns to where you are sitting in a meditative position. Allow the feelings of glory and success to overwhelm you for a minute before you shift your attention back to your physical body, watching your chest rise and fall.

Please practice this exercise over and over until you can do it with your eyes shut. Add to this one with as many as you can find on the internet.

Conclusion

Ernest Agyemang Yeboah once said, "If you fail to control your thought, your thought will never fail to control you! Master the art of controlling your thought better, and your thought will control you better." You have taken the first step in increasing control of your mind by allowing me to share my knowledge with you. I'm proud of you for doing that. The instances when your thoughts have ruled the roost are over. There will be no situations where you fail to find your creativity and master the art of precision anymore. You will be the master of your mind and understand that it's all scientific rather than some magical fantasy.

You are no longer a part of the statistics of men and women who have been enslaved by their neural processes in the brain. They are bound by chains and react to triggers in a wildly inept fashion. They suffer from frequent outbursts that they cannot understand. However, you can stop dreading that meeting tomorrow in which you have to deliver an inspirational speech in front of colleagues. The negative thoughts that housed themselves in your frontal lobe are now under your command. Fear is but a word now, and you won't stand there sweating from every pore anymore. The thoughts that made you cave in public won't hinder you when you set foot on that stage. Feel the power within you when your shoe touches the stage floor.

You will speak with confidence because the memories that swayed your cognitive processes before have been properly dealt with. Your voice will resonate poise over the people in front of you. They will look up to you, and this will encourage them to follow. You can feel the electricity running through your circuitry as the words leave your mouth. You have carefully thought of every word before you stepped up.

The problem is that too many of us suffer from all these distortions in our lives, and they cause us to fail at reaching for the stars. They send us into a frantic panic, and the physical symptoms alone are dreadful. These people's hearts race as they fear the same outcome from a familiar strand in their mind. Anxiety is the face of fear, after all. The same strand of memory draws images that we call thoughts. Negative or dysfunctional thoughts are swift and slip past the conscious awareness of most people's ability to recognize them for what they are.

You have learned about the techniques that can help you witness these intrusive thoughts, and now you understand why you felt the way you did. There's no need to feel like that anymore as you have regained control of your cycle before it hit rock bottom. Science has shown you how the brain works, and biology has explained how each character ratifies with the next. The chemistry involved isn't that complicated. This expansive network is what brings us to the answers we provide our patients in psychology. The mind has always intrigued me, and thought mechanisms are pertinently adaptable.

The practices in this book have helped thousands upon thousands of people, and I've wasted no time in sugar-coating anything. You have a right to know every factor at play in the bondage that has held you back until now. All you have to do is sever the connection that has pulled a veil over your eyes. Continue practicing what you've learned because practice undeniably makes perfect.

You will use the physical and mental exercises I shared with you to regain the steering wheel so that you can accomplish your desires and retrain a complex organism. You deserve your heart's desire for taking a stance against automatic thoughts that permeate through your body and mind. The psychological toolkit that you carry around will prevent any further harm to your self-schema. Don't waste any more time now and go out there to become all you can be.

References

Association for Psychological Science. (September 24, 2012) Retrieved from www.psychologicalscience.org/video/slow-thinking-is-wise-thinking.html

Bergland, C. (December 22, 2018) Negative Moods May Trigger Inflammation. Retrieved from www.psychologytoday.com/us/blog/the-athletes-way/201812/negative-moods-may-trigger-inflammation

Blades, G. (March 24, 2017) How to Take Control of Your Thoughts. Retrieved from https://medium.com/thrive-global/how-to-take-control-of-your-thoughts-5e2e6a9dc22c

Boyd, R. (February 7, 2008) Do People Only Use 10 Percent of Their Brains? Retrieved from www.scientificamerican.com/article/do-people-only-use-10-percent-of-their-brains/

Cambridgeshire and Peterborough National Health Services Foundation Trust. (January, 2019) Retrieved from www.cpft.nhs.uk/PDF/Miscellaneous/Managing%20Thoughts%20and%20Feelings%20CBT%20Booklet%20May%202017.pdf

Chater, N. (July 29, 2018) What We Know About the Human Mind. Retrieved from www.psychologytoday.com/us/blog/the-mind-is-flat/201807/what-we-know-about-the-human-mind

Chen, W. (April 30, 2014) Worried? Slow Thinking May Help You See Things Clearly. Retrieved from www.entrepreneur.com/article/233441

Cherry, K. & Gans, S. (November 4, 2019) Cognitive Psychology: The Science of How We Think. Retrieved from www.verywellmind.com/cognitive-psychology-4157181

Cooper, B.B. (April 1, 2016) 10 Surprising Facts About How Our Brains Work. Retrieved from https://buffer.com/resources/10-surprising-facts-about-how-our-brain-works

Dietrich, C. (2010) Decision Making: Factors that Influence Decision Making, Heuristics Used, and Decision Outcomes. Retrieved from http://www.inquiriesjournal.com/articles/180/2/

decision-making-factors-that-influence-decision-making-heuristics-used-and-decision-outcomes

Goldstein, M. (August 20, 2019) How to Control Your Thoughts and Be the Master of Your Mind. Retrieved from www.lifehack.org/articles/lifestyle/how-to-master-your-mind-part-one-whos-running-your-thoughts.html

Goldwin-Meadow, S. & Beilock, S. (December, 2010) Action's influence on thought: The case of gesture. Retrieved from www.ncbi.nlm.nih.gov/pmc/articles/PMC3093190/

Good Therapy Staff. (April 7, 2015) 20 Cognitive Distortions and How They Affect Your Life. Retrieved from www.goodtherapy.org/blog/20-cognitive-distortions-and-how-they-affect-your-life-0407154

Greenberg, M. (April 2, 2013) Become the CEO of Your Own Brain in Six Easy Steps. Retrieved from www.psychologytoday.com/intl/blog/the-mindful-self-express/201304/become-the-ceo-your-own-brain-in-six-easy-steps

Hampton, D. (March 24, 2017) How Your Thoughts Change Your Brain, Cells and Genes. Retrieved from www.huffpost.com/entry/how-your-thoughts-change-your-brain-cells-and-genes_b_9516176?guccounter=1

Hart, P. & Towey, S. (n.d.) What Is the Mind-Body Connection? Retrieved from www.takingcharge.csh.umn.edu/what-is-the-mind-body-connection

How does the brain work? (October 31, 2018) Retrieved from www.ncbi.nlm.nih.gov/books/NBK279302/

Jabr, F. (December 8, 2011) Cache Cab: Taxi Drivers' Brains Grow to Navigate London's Streets. Retrieved from www.scientificamerican.com/article/london-taxi-memory/

Johnson, J.A. (October 20, 2016) Biology Determines Every Thought, Feeling, and Behavior. Retrieved from www.psychologytoday.com/us/blog/cui-bono/201610/biology-determines-every-thought-feeling-and-behavior

Kringelbach, M.L.; Lehtonen, A.; & Squire, S. et al. (2008) A specific and rapid neural signature for parental instinct. Retrieved from https://journals.plos.org/plosone/article?id=10.13 71/journal.pone.0001664

Lewis, R. (February 24, 2019) What Actually Is a Thought? And How Is Information Physical? Retrieved from www.psychologytoday.com/us/blog/finding-purpose/201902/what-actually-is-thought-and-how-is-information-physical

Maitan-Casalis, W. (n.d.) 5 Things You Need to Know About Your Mind-Body Connection. Retrieved from www.powerofpositivity.com/5-things-need-know-mind-body-connection/

McLeod, S. (2015) Cognitive Psychology. Retrieved from www.simplypsychology.org/cognitive.html

Morcella, E. (February 9, 2012) What Is a Thought? Retrieved from www.psychologytoday.com/us/blog/consciousness-and-the-brain/201202/what-is-thought

Nierhaus, T.; Vidaurre, C.; Sannelli, C.; Mueller, K.R.; & Villringer, A. (November 5, 2019) Can our thoughts alter our brains? Retrieved from www.cbs.mpg.de/Can-our-thoughts-alter-our-brains

Pandya, S.K. (December, 2011) Understanding Brain, Mind and Soul: Contributions from Neurology and Neurosurgery. Retrieved from

www.ncbi.nlm.nih.gov/pmc/articles/PMC3115284
/

Park, N.; Peterson, C.; & Collon, K. (May, 2016) Positive Psychology and Physical Health. Retrieved from www.ncbi.nlm.nih.gov/pmc/articles/PMC6124958 /

Peters, R. (February, 2006) Ageing and the brain. Retrieved from www.ncbi.nlm.nih.gov/pmc/articles/PMC2596698 /

Rackley, M. (October 18, 2016) Mind the gap: the importance of the mind/body connection in physical and mental health. Retrieved from www.counselling-directory.org.uk/memberarticles/mind-the-gap-the-importance-of-the-mindbody-connection-in-physical-and-mental-h

Robison, E. (March 1, 2013) Can We Control Our Thoughts? Why Do Thoughts Pop into My Head as I'm Trying to Fall Asleep? Retrieved from www.scientificamerican.com/article/can-we-control-our-thoughts/

San Francisco State University. (February 3, 2015) Our thoughts are susceptible to external influence, even

against   our   will.   Retrieved   from
www.sciencedaily.com/releases/2015/02/15020314
2309.htm

Stark, E. (July, 2017) Is slowness the essence of
knowledge?   Retrieved   from
https://thepsychologist.bps.org.uk/volume-
30/july-2017/slowness-essence-knowledge

Tanaka, S.; Tani, T.; Ribot, J.; O'Hashi, K.; & Imamura,
K. (April 29, 2009) A Postnatal Critical Period for
Orientation Plasticity in the Cat Visual Cortex.
Retrieved   from
https://journals.plos.org/plosone/article?id=10.13
71/journal.pone.0005380#ack

Troy, A.S.; Wilhelm, F.H.; & Mauss, I.B. (December
2010) Seeing the Silver Lining: Cognitive Reappraisal
Ability Moderates the Relationship Between Stress and
Depressive   Symptoms.   Retrieved   from
www.ncbi.nlm.nih.gov/pmc/articles/PMC3278301
/

Weger, U. & Loughnan, S. (August 19, 2012)
Mobilizing unused resources: Using the placebo
concept to enhance cognitive performance. Retrieved
from
www.tandfonline.com/doi/abs/10.1080/17470218.2
012.751117?journalCode=pqje20#.Ud-Z2o7BHfB

Wells, D. (July 6, 2017) Fun Facts About the Brain You Didn't Know. Retrieved from www.healthline.com/health/fun-facts-about-the-brain#1

Woodward, M. (February 1, 2018) Why Think Time Is So Important in a Distracted World. Retrieved from www.psychologytoday.com/us/blog/spotting-opportunity/201802/why-think-time-is-so-important-in-distracted-world

Worrall, S. (March 17, 2018) Why the Brain-Body Connection Is More Important Than We Think. Retrieved from www.nationalgeographic.com/news/2018/03/why-the-brain-body-connection-is-more-important-than-we-think/